Travel Writing

Selected and edited by
Geoff Barton

Oxford University Press

Oxford University Press, Walton Street, Oxford OX2 6DP

Oxford New York
Athens Auckland Bangkok Bombay
Calcutta Cape Town Dar es Salaam Delhi
Florence Hong Kong Istanbul Karachi
Kuala Lumpur Madras Madrid Melbourne
Mexico City Nairobi Paris Singapore
Taipei Tokyo Toronto

and associated companies in
Berlin Ibadan

Oxford is a trade mark of Oxford University Press

© Selection and activities: Geoff Barton 1993
Reprinted 1994

ISBN 0 19 831283 0

Typeset by Pentacor PLC, High Wycombe, Bucks
Printed and bound in Great Britain by
Butler & Tanner Ltd, Frome and London

Cover illustration by Hamish Blakely

Also available in the *Oxford Literature Resources* series:

Contents

Contents

Acknowledgements

The editor and publisher are grateful for permission to include the following copyright material in this collection.

BBC Enterprises: extract from *Around the World in Eighty Days* by Michael Palin, published by BBC Books at £9.99 in paperback and £15.95 in hardback. **Curtis Brown Ltd.:** 'Wherever I Hang' by Grace Nichols. © Grace Nichols. **Faber & Faber Ltd.:** 'To the Sea' from *High Windows* by Philip Larkin (1974). **The Guardian:** 'My Favourite Places' by Yehudi Menuhin, *Weekend Guardian*; 'Barracuda Breakfast' by Kevin Pilley, *The Guardian*, 12 October 1991; 'Mindless in Gaza' by Jack Shamash, *Weekend Guardian*, 12 October 1991. All © *The Guardian*; Simon Rae, 'Betjemanesque', *The Guardian*, 7 September 1991. (Reprinted by permission of the author.) **Harper Collins Publishers Limited:** extract from *A Traveller's Life* by Eric Newby; extract from Danziger's Travels by Nick Danziger (Paladin, 1988); extract from *Hunting Mr Heartbreak* by Jonathan Raban (Collins Harvill, 1990). **William Heinemann Ltd.:** extract from *Among the Russians* by Colin Thubron. **David Higham Associates:** extact from *The Theory and Practice of Travel* by Keith Waterhouse (Hodder/Coronet, 1989). **Hodder & Stoughton Ltd.:** from *A Traveller on Horseback* by Christina Dodwell (1987). **Charles Hose:** from *The Field Book of a Jungle Wallah* by Charles Hose. Originally published by H. F. & G. Witherby, London 1929. **The Independent:** 'Reasons to be Cheerful' by Frank Barrett, 7 September 1991. **Irish Tourist Board/J. Walter Thompson:** advertisement for West of Ireland. **Jersey Tourism/ Wakefields:** advertisement for Jersey. **John Murray (Publishers) Ltd.:** extract from *A Winter in Arabia* by Freya Stark (1940). **The Observer:** 'Mountain Madness' by John Collee. © *The Observer* 1991. **Smita Patel:** extract from *Between Two Cultures*, reprinted in M. Davies & N. Jansz, *Women, Travel, Adventures, Advice and Experience* (Harrap Colombus, 1990). **Penguin Books Ltd.:** extract from *Into the Heart of Borneo* by Redmond O'Hanlon (1985). **Peters Fraser & Dunlop Group Ltd.:** 'Postcard from Epcot' from *Postcard from Epcot – Flying Visits* by Clive James (Cape/Picador). **Murray Pollinger Ltd.:** extract from 'In the Jungle' by Annie Dillard. © Annie Dillard. **Random House UK Ltd.:** 'The Stowaway' from *A History of the World in 10$^{1/2}$*

Chapters (Cape, 1988); extracts from *Travels on My Elephant* by Mark Shand (Cape, 1991). **Rogers Coleridge & White Ltd.:** extract from *Tracks* by Robyn Davidson (Jonathan Cape/Vintage). **Virago Press:** extract from *A Lady's Life in The Rocky Mountains* by Isabella Bird (1982); extract from *Sequins for a Ragged Hem* by Amryl Johnson (1988). **Greg Ward**: 'When Pele Blows The Lava Flows' from *The Rough Guide: USA* (Harrap Collins, 1992).

In some instances it has not been possible to trace or contact the copyright holder prior to publication. However if notified the publisher will be pleased to rectify any errors or omissions at the earliest opportunity.

The author would also like to thank Deb Bright for her valuable suggestions and advice on the content of this anthology.

Preface

This collection contains a wide variety of travel writing. Some writers focus upon the process of travel itself; others describe the people and places they encounter; some use travel as a form of autobiography; others as a mode of journalism. Travel for some is a pleasurable, eye-opening experience; for others it is uncomfortable, occasionally unbearable. In reflecting a wide range of attitudes and ideas, the anthology is intended to highlight the drawbacks and dangers of travel as well as celebrate the enjoyable and exotic.

There is so much fine travel writing available that selecting and organizing the material has been a stimulating challenge. The five thematic sections – The Art of Travel; Explorers; Travellers; Tourists; and Coming Home – provide a convenient structure. Sometimes, perhaps, the structure proves simplistic; for example it is not always clear whether a writer ought to be deemed 'explorer' or 'traveller'. Readers are welcome to take issue with these categories. They do prove useful, however, in allowing interesting juxtapositions of texts. Within the sections I have frequently placed extracts together which seem to illuminate one another by comparison, by showing different responses to an experience or place, conflicting attitudes, or divergent versions of the same story.

The follow-on activities are intended to stimulate discussion and written responses that will provide a wide range of work to meet many of the requirements of Key Stage 4 and Standard Grade. The activities invite readers to question writers' assumptions and to think more about their own attitudes to travel. Most important of all, they encourage the reader to reflect upon the genre of travel writing itself. Why, after all, should we want to read about someone else's travels? What do other people's journeys tell us about them and about us? How does fiction shape travel experiences differently from non-fiction? Questions like these underpin the follow-on ideas.

Many of the writers may be unfamiliar to readers new to travel writing. I hope that the suggested activities and suggestions for wider reading will provide a starting-point for readers to develop their own routes for exploring this fascinating and growing genre of literature. Bon voyage.

Geoff Barton

The Art of Travel

Mindless in Gaza

Jack Shamash

Here is a speck of comfort for anyone not planning to canoe up the Amazon or trek across Siberia – contrary to what anyone will tell you, travel does not broaden the mind.

It was the Victorians who were really obsessed with travel. They lived at a time when travel really did harden the body and improve the spirit. It took a rare breed of man to trudge through some malaria-infested swamp in a pith helmet, after the native bearers had drunk all the whisky, stolen the bully beef, and run off with the compass.

Since then, travellers have thought of themselves as faintly noble and they look down on mere tourists who stay in comfortable hotels and ride in air-conditioned buses. To travellers it is a mark of pride to suffer as much as possible. They get a perverse joy from spending all day squatting over a sordid cesspit.

Paul Theroux, a best-selling travel writer, is one of the people caught up in the myth: 'The nearest thing to writing a novel is travelling in a strange country.' Travel, he declares, is a creative act. It isn't. It may be fun. It may be interesting, but travellers get no insight into eternal truths.

Travellers learn a lot about shopping (good in Singapore, bad in China). They learn how to avoid the young boys that follow you everywhere in Morocco (look at them with a condescending smile). They discover how to find a *pensione* in Spain; what sort of Mexican food to avoid, or where to buy good hash in Tunisia. In doing so they find out very little about Orientals, Arabs, Spaniards or Mexicans. A knowledge of Indian railway timetables and hotel prices is not the same as understanding Indian culture.

Travellers acquire useless skills, such as how to make trivial conversation with new acquaintances – discussing cameras or makes of car is a sure-fire way of provoking long and boring discussions.

Many people use travel as an idiotic form of escapism. Oxford graduates, who would not be remotely interested in getting to know British working-class people on council estates, find it uplifting to go sightseeing among the poor of the Third World.

The worst travellers are the long-term ones – often people with personal problems who are keen, not so much to see the world, as to avoid returning home. As a rule, the only people who travel for more than a year are simpletons, social inadequates, or New Zealanders.

Travel can sometimes close the mind altogether. I once hitched a lift with a van-load of drunken Aborigines. They had already picked up one hitch-hiker who had been travelling round the world for four years. He had no fixed home and no fixed job and didn't care what his next destination was.

In desperation for something to talk about, I told my fellow traveller that I was going to a famous beauty spot in Queensland. Did he know it? 'Oh yeah,' he said, 'I think there's a good Salvation Army hostel somewhere near there.'

Around the World in Eighty Days

Jules Verne

CHAPTER II

A conversation which could cost Phileas Fogg dear

Phileas Fogg had left his house in Saville Row at 11.30, and having placed his right foot in front of his left five hundred and seventy-five times, and his left in front of his right five hundred and seventy-six times, arrived at the Reform Club, a large building in Pall Mall.

Phileas Fogg went straight to the dining room with its nine windows overlooking a delightful garden, and took his seat at his usual table which was already laid for him. His lunch consisted of an *hors d'œuvre*, boiled fish with Reading Sauce, underdone roast beef stuffed with rhubarb and green gooseberries, and a piece of Cheshire cheese – together with several cups of excellent tea specially imported for the Reform Club.

At 12.47 he rose and went to the smoking room where a club servant handed him the *Times*. The reading of it occupied Phileas Fogg until 3.45, and that of the *Standard* until dinner, after which he reappeared in the smoking room to read the *Morning Chronicle*.

Half an hour later various members of the Reform Club arrived. These were Phileas Fogg's regular partners, fanatical whist players like himself – Andrew Stuart, the engineer, the bankers, John Sullivan and Samuel Fallentin, the brewer, Thomas Flanagan, and Gauthier Ralph, a director of the Bank of England.

'Well, Ralph,' enquired Thomas Flanagan, 'what's happening about the robbery?'

'Oh,' replied Andrew Stuart, 'the Bank will whistle for its money.'

'On the contrary,' said Gauthier Ralph, 'I hope we shall lay hands on the culprit. Police inspectors have been sent to America and the Continent, all the chief ports here are being watched, and it will be difficult for this fellow to escape.'

'Is there a description of the thief, then?' asked Stuart.

'He's not exactly a thief,' replied Ralph seriously.

'What! Not exactly a thief – this character who has taken £55,000 in bank notes?'

'The *Morning Chronicle* assures us that he is a gentleman.'

This remark came from Phileas Fogg, whose head rose from a sea of paper surrounding him to greet his colleagues.

The event under discussion, reported at length in various newspapers, had occurred three days ago on 29th September. A packet of bank notes amounting to £55,000 had been taken from the chief cashier's counter position in the Bank of England. To anyone who expressed astonishment that such a theft could have been pulled off so easily, Gauthier Ralph simply said that at the time the chief cashier was making out a receipt for 3*s*. 6*d*., and one's eyes could not be everywhere at once.

Detectives had been sent to the chief ports at home and abroad with the promise of a reward of £2,000 for the apprehension of the thief, plus five per cent of the sum recovered. Until an enquiry provided more particulars they were to watch all travellers.

However, as the *Morning Chronicle* said, there was reason to believe that the thief was not a member of a gang. On 29th September a gentleman, well-dressed, with good manners and a distinguished air, had been particularly noticed at the counter, and the enquiry produced a fairly definite description of him which was immediately sent to all detectives.

'I maintain,' said Stuart, 'that the chances favour the thief, who must be a pretty smart man.'

'Oh, come now,' replied Ralph, 'there isn't a single country where he can hide.'

'Hmp! The world is big enough,' grunted Stuart.

'It was... once,' murmured Phileas Fogg. 'Cut, please,' he added, pushing the cards towards Flanagan.

The discussion ceased during the rubber, but Andrew Stuart revived it by saying:

'What do you mean – once? Has the world grown smaller by any chance?'

'Undoubtedly,' answered Ralph. 'I agree with Mr Fogg. We can range over it ten times faster than we could a century ago. In the case we are discussing, it will speed up investigations.'

'And make the thief's escape easier!'

'Your turn to play,' said Phileas Fogg.

'But Ralph,' insisted Stuart, 'you have found an odd way of saying the earth has grown smaller. Just because one can go round it in three months... '

'In eighty days only,' said Phileas Fogg.

'True, gentlemen,' added John Sullivan. 'Eighty days – since the completion of the section of the Indian Peninsular Railway between Rothal and Allahabad. Here is the *Morning Chronicle's* calculation:

London-Suez via Mon Cenis and Brindisi	
by rail and boat	7 days
Suez–Bombay – boat	13 "
Bombay–Calcutta – rail	3 "
Calcutta–Hong Kong – boat	13 "
Hong Kong–Yokohama – boat	6 "
Yokohama–San Francisco – boat	22 "
San Francisco–New York – rail	7 "
New York–London – boat and rail	9 "
	80 days

'Oh, yes, eighty days,' cried Stuart, 'but not counting wind, weather, shipwreck, railway accidents and so on.'

'All included,' replied Mr Fogg, continuing his play.

'Theoretically you are right, Mr Fogg, but in practice... '

'In practice as well, Mr Stuart.'

'I'd like to see you do it.'

'It depends on you. Let us set out together.'

'Heaven forbid!' gasped Stuart. 'But I would wager £4,000 that such a journey is impossible.'

'On the contrary, perfectly possible. I will do it.'

'When?'

'At once – but I warn you that it will be at your expense. I have £20,000 on deposit at Baring Bros. I will willingly risk that sum.'

'Twenty thousand pounds,' gasped John Sullivan, 'that you may lose by a single unforeseen delay!'

'The unforeseen does not exist,' replied Phileas Fogg simply.

'But, this period of eighty days is calculated as the minimum time required.'

'A minimum, well used, suffices for everything.'

'But to avoid overstepping it you would have to jump mathematically from train to boat and boat to train.'

'I shall jump mathematically.'

'You're joking!'

'A true-born Englishman never jokes when such a serious thing as a wager is concerned,' replied Phileas Fogg. 'I wager £20,000 against any takers that I will make the journey round the world in eighty days, that is, one thousand, nine hundred and twenty hours, or one hundred and fifteen thousand, two hundred minutes. Do you accept the challenge?'

'We accept,' replied Stuart, Fallentin, Sullivan, Flanagan and Ralph.

'Good,' said Mr Fogg. 'The train for Dover leaves at eight forty-five. I shall take it.'

'This evening?' asked Stuart.

'This evening,' replied Phileas Fogg. 'Since to-day is Wednesday, 2nd October, I should be back in London in this smoking room of the Reform Club on Saturday, 21st December, at eight forty-five in the evening, in default of which the £20,000 to my credit at Baring Bros. will belong to you. Here is a cheque for that sum.'

The details of the wager were drawn up in legal form and signed by the six gentlemen.

Phileas Fogg remained calm. He had pledged half of his fortune only as he foresaw that he might have to expend the remainder in the execution of this difficult, if not impossible, project.

The clock struck seven and it was suggested to Mr Fogg that whist should be abandoned to allow him to prepare for his departure.

'I am always prepared,' replied that unruffled gentleman. 'I lead a diamond. Your play, Mr Stuart.'

CHAPTER XXIV

In which are related various incidents which could take place only on American Railroads

The same evening the train continued without further hindrance, passed Fort Saunders, crossed the Cheyenne Pass, and reached Evans Pass. Here the railroad reached its highest point, 8,091 feet above sea-level. From here the passengers had only to descend to the Atlantic.

In three nights and three days 1,382 miles had been covered since leaving San Francisco. Four nights and four days should be sufficient to reach New York. Phileas Fogg was, therefore, keeping to his timetable. At eleven o'clock the train entered the state of Nebraska, passed near Sedgwick, and touched Julesburgh on the southern branch of the Platte River.

It was at this point that the inauguration of the Union Pacific Railroad took place on 23rd October, 1867. Here two powerful locomotives pulling nine cars of invited guests came to a halt. Cheers rang out, Sioux and Pawnee Indians enacted a small tribal war, fireworks burst in the sky, and finally, printed on a portable printing press, the first number of the *Railway Pioneer* was published.

At eight o'clock in the morning Fort MacPherson was left behind and the one hundred and first meridian was crossed.

Mr Fogg and his partners had taken up their game again. None of them complained of the length of the journey – not even

7

the dummy. Fix had begun by winning several guineas which he was now in process of losing, but he showed himself to be no less fervent than Mr Fogg. During the morning luck seemed to favour the latter gentleman. Aces and honours rained from his hands. At one moment he was about to play a spade when, from behind his seat a voice was heard saying: 'I guess I should play a diamond.'

Mr Fogg, Mrs Aouda and Fix raised their heads. Colonel Proctor was standing close by. Stamp Proctor and Phileas Fogg recognized each instantly.

'Ah! So it's you, limey,' said the colonel. 'It's you who's going to play a spade.'

'And who plays it,' replied Mr Fogg coldly, throwing down a ten.

'Well, I'd rather play a diamond,' retorted the colonel, and he made a move to pick up the card which had been played, adding, 'You don't know the first thing about the game.'

'Perhaps I shall be more competent at another,' answered Mr Fogg, rising to his feet.

'It's up to you to try it, you John Bull mongrel,' replied the coarse-mannered specimen.

Mrs Aouda had grown pale as the blood drained from her face. She seized the arm of Mr Fogg who pushed her away gently. Passepartout was ready to fling himself on the American, who was staring at his adversary in a more insolent manner than ever, when Fix rose to his feet, and moving towards Colonel Proctor said:

'You forget, sir, that it is me with whom you have to settle, me whom you not only insulted but struck.'

'Mr Fix,' said Mr Fogg, 'I beg your pardon, but this concerns me alone. In asserting that I was wrong in playing a spade the colonel insulted me afresh, and he will give me satisfaction for it.'

'When you like, where you like, and with what weapons you like,' answered the American.

Mrs Aouda tried in vain to hold Mr Fogg back. The inspector tried without success to take up the quarrel on his own account, and Passepartout wanted to throw the colonel out of the door, but a sign from his master stopped him. Phileas Fogg left the car and the American followed him on to the platform.

'Sir,' said Mr Fogg to his opponent, 'I am in a great hurry to return to Europe and any delay would be detrimental to my interests.'

'What the hell's that got to do with me?' answered the colonel.

'Sir,' continued Mr Fogg, very politely, 'after our meeting in San Francisco I conceived the plan of returning to find you in America as soon as I had completed the business which calls me to the Old World.'

'You don't say!'

'Will you name a place where we can meet in six months' time?'

'Why not six years?'

'I said six months,' replied Mr Fogg, 'and I shall be at the agreed spot at the agreed time exactly.'

'Moonshine!' jeered Stamp Proctor. 'Now or never.'

'So be it,' answered Mr Fogg. 'Are you going to New York?'

'No.'

'To Chicago? Omaha?'

'None of your business. D'you know Plum Creek?'

'No,' said Mr Fogg.

'It's the next station. The train'll be there in an hour. Stops ten minutes. In ten minutes we can exchange shots.'

'Agreed,' answered Mr Fogg. 'I shall halt there.'

'Ha! You'll stop there more likely!' sneered the American with unparalleled insolence.

'Who can tell, sir?' replied Mr Fogg, and returned to his seat as unruffled as usual.

There the gentleman began to reassure Mrs Aouda, telling her that mere blustering need never be feared. He then asked Fix to be his second. Fix could hardly refuse, and Mr Fogg took up the interrupted game, playing a spade with perfect calmness.

At eleven o'clock a whistle from the engine signalled the approach to Plum Creek Station. Mr Fogg rose, and followed by Fix went out on to the car platform. Passepartout accompanied him carrying a brace of revolvers. Mrs Aouda remained in the car, pale as death.

At the same moment the door of the next car opened and Colonel Proctor appeared on the platform followed by his second, a Yankee of the same stamp. Just as the two adversaries were about to step down on the track the guard came running up calling:

'No one gets out, gentlemen.'

'And why not?' demanded the colonel.

'We're twenty minutes behind,' replied the guard, 'and we leave at once. There's the bell.'

The bell sounded and the train began to move.

'Very sorry, gentlemen,' said the guard. 'Any other time I'd have obliged you. But after all, if you haven't time to fight here what's to stop you fighting while we're going along?'

'Perhaps that won't suit this gentleman,' sneered the colonel.

'It will suit me perfectly,' answered Phileas Fogg.

'My word! We're in America all right,' thought Passepartout. 'And the guard is a real gentleman.'

The two principals and their seconds, preceded by the guard passing from one car to another, made their way to the rear of the train. The last car was occupied only by ten passengers or so and the guard asked them if they would be so good as to vacate it for a few minutes as two gentlemen wished to settle an affair of honour. The occupants were only too happy to oblige the gentlemen and retired to the platforms.

This car, about fifty feet long, lent itself admirably to the event. The two opponents could advance towards each other between the rows of seats and let fly at their ease. Never had a duel been so easy to arrange. Mr Fogg and Colonel Proctor, each provided with a six-shot revolver, entered the car and their seconds shut the doors. At a whistle from the engine they would begin to shoot. Then, after a period of two minutes, what remained of the two gentlemen would be removed from the car.

Really nothing could be simpler. It was, in fact, so simple that Fix and Passepartout felt their hearts thumping as though they would burst.

All were waiting for the blast of the whistle when suddenly wild shouts rang out, accompanied by the sound of shots – but these did not come from the duellists' car. The shots, on the contrary, occurred at the front of and along the whole length of the train, and shrieks of fear came from the interior of the cars. Colonel Proctor and Mr Fogg, revolver in hand, immediately left the car and rushed forward to the point from which most of the noise and the shots were coming. They had realized that the train was being attacked by a band of Sioux.

These daring Indians were not making a first attempt, but more than once had stopped trains. Following their custom, about a hundred of them, not waiting for the train to stop, but hurling themselves on to the steps, climbed into the cars like clowns scrambling on to horses going at full gallop.

The Sioux had guns – hence the shots to which the passengers, almost all of whom were armed, replied with revolver shots. The Indians had first leapt on to the engine where the driver and the stoker were knocked senseless. A Sioux chief, trying to stop the train but not understanding how to manage the regulator handle, had opened it instead of closing it, and the engine running wild reached a frightful speed.

At the same time the Sioux had attacked the cars. They ran like maddened apes along the roofs, forced open the doors, and fought hand to hand with the passengers. From the baggage car, broken open and pillaged, luggage was hurled on to the track while shouts and shots continued without a break.

The passengers defended themselves bravely. Some cars with barricaded doors withstood a siege, like moving forts carried along at one hundred miles an hour.

From the very beginning of the attack Mrs Aouda had borne herself bravely. Revolver in hand she had defended herself with spirit, firing through the broken windows whenever an Indian showed himself. About twenty dead Sioux had fallen by the side of the track and the wheels passed over others who slipped from the platforms between the cars. Many of the passengers, seriously wounded by bullets or tomahawks, sprawled on the seats.

11

The battle had already gone on for ten minutes and could only finish to the advantage of the Sioux unless the train were stopped. In fact Fort Kearney, where there was a section of American troops, was only two miles away, but once Fort Kearney was passed the Sioux would be masters of the train until the next station was reached.

The guard was fighting alongside Mr Fogg when he was hit by a bullet. As he fell he groaned:

'We're lost if the train doesn't stop in five minutes.'

'It shall stop,' said Mr Fogg who prepared to dash out of the car.

'Stay here, sir,' cried Passepartout. 'This is my job.'

Phileas Fogg had no chance to stop Passepartout who, opening a door without being seen by the Indians, managed to crawl under the car. And then, while bullets criss-crossed above him, hanging on to chains, helping himself with brake rods and girders, he clambered from one car to another with marvellous agility and finally reached the front of the train unseen.

Once there, hanging with one hand between the baggage car and the tender, he unhooked the safety chains, but because of the pull he would never have been able to unhitch the coupling had not a sudden jolt from the engine made it jump. The cars gradually dropped behind while the engine, freed from their weight, leaped ahead with increased speed.

Under their own momentum the cars ran on for some minutes, but the brakes were wound on from inside and finally the train stopped less than a hundred yards from Kearney Station.

To this point soldiers from the fort had run at full speed on hearing the shots. The Sioux had not waited for them and before the cars had stopped the whole band had disappeared.

But when the passengers held a roll-call on the platform they found that some failed to answer to their names, and among these was the brave Frenchman whose courage had saved them.

Around the World in Eighty Days

Michael Palin

Day 1
25 September

I leave the Reform Club, Pall Mall, London one hundred and fifteen years three hundred and fifty-six days, ten and three-quarter hours after Phileas Fogg. It's a wet, stuffy morning, I've had three and a half hours sleep and the only thing I envy Phileas is that he's fictional.

Few buildings could be more fitted to a Great Departure. With its 60-foot-high main hall, marble columns, galleried arcades and the grand scale of a Renaissance palace the Reform Club is a place of consequence, grand and grave enough to add weight to any venture.

This morning it smells of old fish, and glasses and bottles from the night before stand around. I can see no one sampling the sort of breakfast Fogg had taken the day he left: ' . . . a side dish, a boiled fish with Reading sauce of first quality, a scarlet slice of roast beef garnished with mushrooms, a rhubarb and gooseberry tart, and a bit of Chester cheese, the whole washed down with a few cups of that excellent tea, specially gathered for the stores of the Reform Club.'

I have tried to follow Fogg's example and travel light. 'Only a carpetbag,' he had instructed his servant Passepartout, 'in it two woollen shirts and three pairs of stockings... my mackintosh and travelling cloak, also stout shoes, although we shall walk but little or not at all.' I've managed to find a passable equivalent of a carpet bag and in it packed six shirts, six pairs of socks, six pairs of underpants, three T-shirts, a towel, a pair of swimming trunks, a short-sleeved sweater, three pairs of light trousers (long), two pairs ex-R.A.F. trousers (short), a pair of sports shorts, a sponge bag, various pharmaceuticals, a change of shoes, a jacket and tie, a Sony Walkman, six cassettes, a small short-wave radio, a Panama hat and one or two heavy and serious books with which to improve my mind on long sea journeys. In a shoulder bag I carry my diary, a small dictaphone recorder for on-the-spot notes, a camera, the BBC's *Get By In Arabic*, a Kingsley Amis novel, some extra-strong mints, a packet of 'Family Wipes', an address book and an inflatable globe to enable me to check on our progress. Phileas Fogg would doubtless have regarded all this as clutter, but it's still less than I would take on a two-week holiday.

These bags I heave up onto my shoulders as the clock shows ten o'clock. I carry them down the stairs, out of the tall doorway and into Pall Mall. I've eighty days left to get back in again.

Fogg went from the Reform Club to Charing Cross station, I leave from Victoria.

Here I find Passepartout, who will travel everywhere with me. Unlike Fogg's Passepartout, mine is five people, has fifty pieces of baggage and works for the BBC. Roger Mills is the director of this first leg of the journey and is already bemoaning the fact that we've just missed some foul weather in the English Channel. 'If only this had been yesterday.' He draws on his pipe despondently. Ann Holland is his Production Assistant. She will keep full details of all the shots we take, and keep in touch with our base camp in London. Nigel Meakin and Julian Charrington are the camera team and Ron Brown is recording sound. The film equipment is in containers of many shapes and sizes and mostly very heavy. As I help them down the platform with a muscle-tearing case of film stock I think of Phileas – 'one of those mathematically exact people... never hurried... calm, phlegmatic, with a clear eye' – and how desperately unlike him I am.

However, I am leaving London in a manner of which he would doubtless have approved had it been available in 1872, aboard the Venice-Simplon Orient Express. Last farewells and a check on the exact time of departure by two friends acting as judges. Fogg's friends were bankers. Mine, Messrs Jones and Gilliam, are Pythons. Terry Jones eyes Passepartout, already about his business with the camera. 'You're going to have to look happy for eighty days.' 'No,' I reassure him. 'There'll be no cheating.' Then the whistle sounds, the last door slams and we're off.

Day 66
29 November

At seven o'clock I pull aside the curtains and look out on a silvery-grey morning. A light covering of snow lies between the tracks as we ease into Salt Lake City.

Fogg came here to 'the curious Mormon country' on the 6 December, his 65th day out of London. I'm only a day behind now, after the *Garnet* crossed the Pacific ten days faster than the *General Grant*. On my 66th day I find myself in Passepartout's footsteps, climbing down onto the platform 'to take the air'. The 6 December 1872 and 29 November 1988 sound much the same. 'The weather was cold, the sky grey, but it had stopped snowing. The disc of the sun, enlarged by the mist, looked like an enormous piece of gold, and Passepartout was busy calculating its value in pounds sterling... '

Plenty of time at Salt Lake City this morning to calculate the value of the hazy sun as we are waiting for a connecting train from Seattle which is reported stuck in a snowdrift high in the mountains. The Seattle train, known as the Pioneer, combines here with the California Zephyr from San Francisco and the Desert Wind to form the California Zephyr service to Chicago. We are thirteen cars long when we eventually pull out of Salt Lake City, with three diesel locomotives to haul us up and over the Rockies.

One thing I do miss from Fogg's days are the bison. 'About three o'clock in the afternoon a herd of ten or twelve thousand blocked the railroad. The engine... tried to plunge its spur into the flank of the immense column, but it had to stop before the impenetrable mass.'

The landscape we're travelling through has long been rid of bison and Sioux and Pawnees too, but it's a spectacular backdrop for a bacon and egg breakfast, with snow-sprinkled fields in deep shadow and sun-capped mountains in sharp contrast behind. The train snakes its way into the Rockies following half-frozen streams up curving valleys that are narrowing and steepening all the time. The rocks have been folded and faulted and weathered into tortured crumbling shapes. Pinnacles and boulders rest on tiny stems, there are precarious overhangs and knobbly stacks.

Into the small town of Helper, Utah, about mid-morning. Helper is one of those functional names that abound in this literal, pioneering part of America. Towns with names like Parachute, Rifle, Gypsum, Carbondale and Basalt, Colorado.

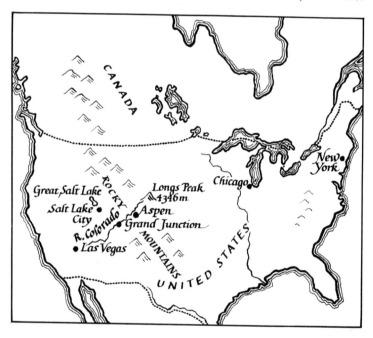

Helper was where additional locomotives required to help trains on the final assault of the Rockies were housed. The town, built for the railway crews, is now a coal-mining centre and has upgraded itself to Helper City.

Early lunch as we pull into Grand Junction Colorado. Elevation 4906 feet. Confluence of the Colorado and Gunnison Rivers. The chief steward, improbably called Abdul Mahmoud, exhorts his team of waiters in the fine art of service: 'Come on. Get 'em in here.'

Today's lunch menu features the forbidden delights of 'The Hot Open Face Sandwich. Your attendant will describe this to you.'

The sun spills into the train as we set off again alongside the Colorado River. It's about 25 yards wide here, and on its flat banks, protected from the winds, grow orchards of apple, pear and peach. Halfway down the train is an observation car. It's filling up fast on this clear and sunny afternoon.

There's a lady of late middle-age calling herself Mar-Mer, who became a clown two years ago. She sparkles with the delight of it all and bursts into songs and jokes with the zeal of a new convert. How does her husband cope with her new profession, I ask. 'Oh... he's kind of an introvert,' she reveals, as if describing an incurable illness. There's a man travelling with his son simply because he prefers trains: 'Sure knocks heck outta driving.' His wife is a cellist with the gloriously named Mile High Orchestra in Denver. But I get the feeling these are not average Americans. They're people who care about their environment, who despise and fear what big business is doing to it and who are immensely knowledgeable about where they live and determined to protect it from unnecessary development.

Back to my seat and doze a little. The mother of the Colorado couple sings to her daughter, in a soft and lilting voice. 'Freight Train', 'When Johnny Comes Marching Home', and others. The combination of this gentle voice and the wide empty country by the winding river is enchanting.

The PA system has become a staff intercom as well as a passenger information service this afternoon. 'Get your cameras ready for some truly great photos' is followed abruptly by a breathless shout of 'Earl, come to the dining car. We need you bad!'

At a quarter to four we reach Glenwood Springs. Elevation 5600 feet. I must take a decision. However short of time I am, I cannot go through the Rockies without a pause to look around. To travel and see nothing is my complaint about aeroplanes, and I can feel myself falling into the same trap. I alight here for a detour which I hope I can afford.

Whilst there's some light left I take a dip in the Glenwood Hot Springs – geothermal waters that soothed the Ute Indians a hundred years ago and beyond. Today they're part of a busy health spa peppered with notices – rules and signs and health warnings in thorough but bewildering American style. The waters, at 104 degrees Fahrenheit, are in the open air, which is currently 35 degrees Fahrenheit. My body quite enjoys this schizophrenic experience. Passepartout sets up on the side of the pool to witness my immersion, but the cloud of steam is so dense that the camera can't find me.

Then drive up to Aspen, about an hour away and two and a half thousand feet up into the Rockies. It's a sort of Christmassy Beverly Hills, but though it may be Californian in income it's East Coast in taste. To the Hotel Jerome whose placid 1889 brick exterior masks an exuberance of Victorian excess inside.

My room is wide and well-furnished in impeccable recreation of the Naughty Nineties. I take a long, slow bath in a room floored in Carrara marble. Then in one of those cultural cross-connections that have characterized the journey I end up picking my way through the snow to a Mexican restaurant, walking through the neat streets of Aspen, treading carefully along icy sidewalks. The unfamiliar feel of ice cold air on my face is very refreshing. Nothing brash or strident intrudes on the rows of carefully maintained houses. No sodium or neon lights allowed here. The town feels like a village, intimate and enclosed.

A last look out of the curtains at midnight. On the ski slopes behind the town, huge machines hurl white plumes of artificial snow onto the mountain.

Hunting Mr Heartbreak

Jonathan Raban

Jonathan Raban set off in 1988 to follow the journey of emigrants from Europe to the New World. On board the *Atlantic Conveyor*, he awaits an approaching hurricane...

I climbed up to the darkened bridge, from where the sea was looking more like a real sea now. The wind had started to cry in the rigging and in the tall stalks of the radar antennae. The anemometer showed fifty-five knots, dead on the nose – or about forty knots of true wind, a full gale.

I made myself a mug of coffee in the chart-room at the back of the bridge. A fax machine was stuttering out a silver weather-map of the Atlantic. On another day, in another vessel, this brittle, smudgy document would have reduced me to panic and a desperate run for a safe harbour.

Captain Jackson came in, scanned the map, and said, 'Yes, looks as if we might be in for a bit of a blow in a day or two... This hurricane here – ' he pointed somewhere down in the region of Bermuda, 'Helene... seems to be changing direction now. See, she was going along this track, westwards; now she's started to head north. We'll be keeping an eye on her over the next few days.' He spoke of this hurricane as indulgently as a teacher might have spoken of a mildly naughty child in their class. I didn't at all like the look of Helene; she was a dense black stain, with her isobars coiled as tightly as the loops of a watch-spring.

'Very probably she'll peter out long before she gets to us. She'll just be another low, like the one we're in.'

I thought, forty degrees to port, forty degrees to starboard, wave tops higher than the bridge, engine failure, caught broadside...

At lunch the next day, both Helen and Wee Helen were white-faced and queasy. Wee Helen was staring into her plate of oxtail soup as if she'd just noticed a hatch of mosquito larvae wriggling about in it. The captain was trying to introduce a more cheerful note.

'It looks as if we'll have a lovely day tomorrow – there's a nice ridge of high pressure coming up. We'll have lost this wind by the evening, and after that we should have a flat calm for a day at least. Lots of sunshine. You'll be able to take those folding loungers out on to the afterdeck and put in some sunbathing time...'

Water slopped in the jug. A spoon slid across the table under its own steam. Wee Helen headed for her cabin, making swimming motions as she floundered up the slope of the dining-room floor.

'It's not the rolling I mind,' her mother said. 'It's this pitching I can't stand. Anyway, like I always say on every voyage, this is *definitely* the last time.'

'Is that a threat or a promise?' said her husband, tucking, with unkind gusto, into his plate of bangers and mash.

'What about the other Helen?' I asked the captain.

'Oh – Helene, you mean? They demoted her this morning. They've got her down to a tropical storm now. I don't think she's going to be any serious problem.' But there was a note in his voice which suggested that he might be putting a comforting gloss on the facts for Mrs Meek's benefit. After lunch I sneaked a look at the latest print-out from the fax machine.

TROPICAL STORM 'HELENE' 37.5N 47.0W EXPECTED 47.5N 37W BY 30/0600 GMT. THEN BECOMING EXTRA-TROPICAL BUT REMAINING A VERY INTENSE STORM, EXPECTED 58N 26W, 950 BY 0100 GMT, 63N, 19W UNCHANGED BY 0200 GMT, 67N 07W 960 BY 03/000 GMT. BRACKNELL W'FAX.

At 950 millibars, the atmospheric pressure of Helene's heart was very low indeed – a hungry vacuum trying to fill itself by sucking in the surrounding air and making it spin, counter-clockwise, like a plug-hole draining water from a bath. This whirling mass of unstable air, with winds of seventy-five to ninety knots at its centre, was moving north-east up the Atlantic at about twenty-five miles an hour. The *Conveyor*, on her Great Circle course to Nova Scotia, was heading on what looked to me like a probable collision-course with angry Helene, whose temper, according to the forecast, was declining from hysterical to just plain furious. Before hurricanes achieved sexual equality (Helene had been preceded, a fortnight before, by Gilbert, who had wrecked the West Indies and torn a broad swathe through northern Mexico), they used to be called 'whirlygirls'. The more closely I looked at the chart, spreading the points of a pair of dividers between where we were and where Helene was going, the more suspicious I became that we had a firm date with a whirlygirl.

...Hurricanes, or tropical cyclones, are hatched in the Cape Verde Basin, ten degrees or more north of the Equator, off the coasts of Senegal, Guinea, Sierra Leone. They feed on moisture from the sea, charging themselves with water that has been warmed over the tropical summer. As this water vapour condenses in the air it releases energy in the form of heat, and the infant hurricane begins to spin. Moving like a top across the surface of the Atlantic, it crosses the Fifteen Twenty Fracture Zone and the Barracuda Ridge, gaining speed and confidence as it goes. By the time it hits the Puerto Rican Trench, it is a mature storm with a name of its own (given to it by NOAA, the happy acronym of the National Oceanic and Atmospheric Administration of the United States). Here, it either keeps on going west into the Caribbean or, like Helene, swerves north and east up the middle of the ocean, where the coldness of the sea usually reduces it to a tame Atlantic Depression.

Helene had more stamina than most of her kind. She was now past the fortieth parallel, but the weather-fax machine was still reporting winds of seventy-five knots at her centre (a hurricane-force wind starts at sixty-four knots). We were more than 300 miles away from her now, but inching closer, our speed reduced by half. The *Conveyor*'s anemometer was showing fifty to fifty-five knots of true wind, as the ship bullied her tonnage through the sea.

Trying to sleep, I was unpleasantly teased by the image of the *Conveyor* as a giant Italian bread-stick. She was so long, so slender, so brittle – why couldn't the waves simply snap her between their fingers? Then she turned into a shunting train. For some reason best known to himself, the driver was ramming the buffers, again and again and again. Then she became my own boat, a cork on a billow, and the slow recollection of her actual tonnage, her huge and ponderous stability at sea, worked on me like a shot of Valium. I woke only when I found myself sliding, half in, half out of the bed.

It was still dark. The ship was leaning over to starboard, pinned there by the steady brunt of the wind. A cautious uphill walk to Officer B's picture window turned out to be an unrewarding exercise. It was impossible to see out for the gluey rime of wet salt on the pane.

Up on the bridge, I found that someone had broken the captain out of his glass box, for he was standing by the wheel in slippers, pyjamas and dressing-gown.

'Morning,' he treated me to a polite nod. 'Bit of a windy morning we've got today.' Slow-smiling, slow-moving, comfortably wrapped in paisley, Captain Jackson had the knack of conjuring around himself a broad ambit of suburban calm and snugness. Far from piloting his ship through the remains of a hurricane on the North Atlantic, he might have been pottering among the geraniums in his greenhouse on the morning of the local flower-show.

'Didn't you sleep well?'

'Fine,' I said, doing my best to match his tone. 'I just wanted to see what was going on up here.'

'There's nothing much to see. We're down to five knots at present. The wind's come up to about sixty.'

The howl somewhere behind and below us was the ship's screw, taking a brief airing out of the water.

I tried to interest the captain in the drama of the storm. I told him of Dickens's passage in January 1842, when the *Britannia* steam-ship had met weather so bad that Thackeray had suspected Dickens of making it up for literary effect. On his own

Atlantic crossing, Thackeray had put his doubts to the captain of his ship and been told that the *Britannia* had indeed been lucky to have survived one of the most famously awful storms on record. I quoted Dickens's magnificent description of being tumbled about in a small ship on a wild sea:

> The water-jug is plunging and leaping like a lively dolphin; all the smaller articles are afloat, except my shoes, which are stranded on a carpet-bag, high and dry, like a couple of coal-barges. Suddenly I see them spring into the air, and behold the looking-glass, which is nailed to the wall, sticking fast upon the ceiling. At the same time the door entirely disappears, and a new one is opened in the floor. Then I begin to comprehend that the state-room is standing on its head.
>
> Before it is possible to make any arrangements at all compatible with this novel state of things, the ship rights. Before one can say 'Thank Heaven!' she wrongs again.

'Yes,' Captain Jackson said. 'It's good. It's... vivid. But when he says *wrongs*, that's not a nautical term he's using there. *Righting herself*, yes; *wronging herself* – no, I don't think you'll find that term has ever been used at sea. It gives away the fact that he wasn't really a seaman, doesn't it?'

With this unanswerable piece of scholarship, the captain went back to glooming over the wheel.

In the chart-room, the barograph was bottoming-out at 994. Helene's centre, about 250 miles off, was supposed to be 950, so we were on the rim of a deep cone of pressure. Five miles to a millibar is a very steep gradient in a weather system. On the faxed map of the Atlantic, it looked as if we'd sailed into a black hole in the ocean, with the isobars packed so tightly together that you couldn't see the gaps between them. I scanned the deck log, to see if the captain was holding out on me, but the only entry in the 'Comments' column was *Pitching easily*, which seemed a characteristically Jacksonian description of our thundering ride over this warm, alpine sea.

All day, and for the most of the next night, the wind stayed up at storm-force, but it was veering. It slowly hauled itself round from south to south-west and then to west, as Helene went north ahead of us, and these shifts confused the sea. The waves began to pile up on top of each other's shoulders. They crashed into each other and exploded into pyramids of froth. By noon, the ship was forced to heave-to. With her engine slowed and her bows pointed up to the weather, she lay in the sea like an enormous log, making no progress over the ground at all.

There were few takers for lunch. The ship's kitchen sounded like a poorly conducted steel band. An incoming tide of gravy washed over the edge of the plate and made a black pool on the table-cloth. I asked the chief engineer how his wife and daughter were.

'They're both got their sheets pulled over their heads and they've turned their faces to the wall.'

In the tropical aquarium, the fish were having a bad time. Most of their habitat had been uprooted from its floor of coloured gravel and now floated on the surface of the water, which was slopping about and spilling over on to the floor. The big striped angel-fish was beating on the glass with its fins, its mouth framing round O's of panic as it tried to recover its lost equilibrium.

Lying hove-to is a state of mind. You mark time in a world that tilts and slides a lot but is going nowhere. You can't remember when it wasn't like this and you can see no particular reason why there should ever be an end to it. The tangled, shaggy ocean strikes you as the ultimate emblem of meaningless activity. For as far as you can see, it goes on heaping itself up and pulling itself to bits. There is something profoundly numbing in the monotonous grandeur of the thing. Staring at it makes you feel as empty-headed as the angel-fish.

A Winter in Arabia

Freya Stark

On the last day in the first week of November, 1937, we flew eastward from Aden, in a cool air filled with early sunlight, a honey light over the sandy shore.

We flew with the Indian Ocean on our right, puckered in motionless ripples, and upon it the broad white roadway of the sun. Seen from so high, the triple, lazy, lace-like edge of waves crept slowly; they did not turn all at once, but unrolled from end to end in a spiral motion, as it were the heart of a shell unwinding. Our aeroplane hung over the azure world with silver wings.

We moved eastward even as the great globe below imperceptibly moved, and were gaining on its circular horizon. Sharks far down were dimly visible, so limpid was the water; small black boats, pointed at either end, were out with their fishermen near the shore; a village or two, earth-coloured huts unnoticeable but for the fields around them, took shelter here and there from wind and sand. On our right the unfurrowed ocean, marked like a damascened blade; on our left the gaunt, leopard-coloured lands, equally lonely; and above, or rather around us, joyous, vivid, and infinite, the skyey spaces loud with our engine, which, like many a mechanical mind, listens to its own voice alone in the silence of creation.

Beyond Shuqra, an ancient flood of lava pours to the sea. Heavy as dough, it rolls into deep water; craters with ruined edges are scattered among its folds. Northward, beyond its bleak and pock-marked slope, stands the high level of Kaur, a wall unbroken. The lava stream is past; the shore flattens out again for many miles; we quiver over the bay of the Fish-eaters, whose coasts, if we could see them close, are scattered with empty

heaps of shells where their descendants still enjoy an ocean
meal. The mountains again approach. A white table-land of
limestone meets black volcanic ridges; sand drifts over all the
landscape; it piles itself in blinding dunes where the great
Meifa'a wadi sweeps to sea; it makes pale foot-hill ranges of its
own, and covers with its shifting carpet the ancient floor of lavas.
Here somewhere the frankincense road, the Arabian highway,
came to the sea and found a crater-built harbour where the
volcanic headlands lie, since there is no other commodity for
shipping along the shallow strips of shore. We look down
eagerly, for we mean later to investigate these inlets. Bal Haf is
there, three small square towers on an infinitesimal, hook-like
bay facing west. The lava-ridge runs in snouts beyond it; an
empty crater, round and perfect, stands like a buttress and forms
another inlet. I marvel to see no trace of ruins here, and only find
out the reason months later, as I ride along the coast: there is no
water.

But a great bay opens beyond, an amphitheatre of volcanoes
and drift-sand, and in it another crater-buttress at the water's
edge with markings like walls upon it, and the little square town
of Bir Ali. Here, I later came to think, is the town of Cana: but
now, as we fly over, we can take our choice of craters; one of
them sticks out to sea like the horns of a crescent moon black in
eclipse. Two islands, one black, one white with the droppings of
gulls, lie in water misty with sunlight; they are the landmarks for
Cana, given by that good mariner who wrote the Periplus nearly
two thousand years ago.

And now we have passed Ras Kelb and Ras Burum, the fire-
twisted ridges are past. Mukalla is in the distance, gathered at
the foot of its hill; and our aeroplane, slowing obliquely, sinks to
the landing-ground of Fuwa. Jusuf, who presides over landings,
is there to meet us, a Buddha figure suddenly active: the young
American who has come to look for oil is there, in a new Dodge,
that races us over the sand. The sea makes a gay splashing, as if
its solitary fields too were meant to be a playground: a million
bubbles shine in the sun at the breaking edge of waves, tossed
like lace frills on a petticoat; crabs, innumerable as water drops,

slide from before our approaching car; until we come to fishermen, who walk barefoot along the hard wet shore and carry on a yoke their baskets of fish – we come to the camel park near the estuary which now lies full of water; through the pointed stone arch of the gateway, by the guardhouse where Yafe'i mercenaries play at dice; to the home of the Resident Adviser.

Explorers

Travels in Harrods

Eric Newby

To me Harrods was not a shop. It was, apart from being the place where I had my hair cut, a whole fascinating world, entirely separate from the one that I normally inhabited. It was a world that, although finite in its extent (it covered thirteen acres), I never explored completely, never could, because although at the early age of which I am writing I did not realize this, it was one in which fresh vistas were constantly being revealed, as the management either opened up new, sometimes ephemeral departments or introduced innovations within existing ones.

For instance, in 1929, following Lindberg's solo crossing of the Atlantic, they opened up an Aviation Department and taught some of their customers to fly. Eventually, when there were not enough potential aviators left untaught among their customers to make it worthwhile keeping it open, it quietly faded away.

'Hold my hand tight, or you'll get lost,' my mother used to say, as she moved through the store, browsing here and there like some elegant ruminant, a gazelle perhaps, or else walking more purposefully if she was on her way to some specific destination, as she often was. My mother was not the sort of person who only entered Harrods in order to shelter from the rain. Once she was in it, she was there as a potential buyer.

And I did hold tight. Get lost in Harrods and you had every chance, I believed, in ending up in the equivalent of that undiscovered country from whose bourne no traveller returns, which when I became a grown-up with an account of my own I located somewhere between Adjustments and Personal Credit (which comprehended Overdue Accounts) and the Funeral

Department for those whose shopping days were done but whose credit was still good, both of which were on the fourth floor.

This world, which I was forced to regard from what was practically floor level, was made up of the equivalents of jungles, savannas, mountains, arctic wastes and even deserts. All that was lacking were seas and lakes and rivers, although at one time I distinctly remember there being some kind of fountain. The jungles were the lavish displays of silk and chiffon printed with exotic fruits and lush vegetation in which I was swallowed up as soon as I entered Piece Goods, on the ground floor, which made the real Flower Department seem slightly meagre by contrast. The biggest mountains were in the Food Halls, also on the ground floor, where towering ranges and isolated stacks of the stuff rose high above me, composed of farmhouse Cheddars, Stiltons, *foie gras* in earthenware pots, tins of biscuits, something like thirty varieties of tea and at Christmas boxes of crackers with wonderful fillings (musical instruments that really worked, for instance), ten-pound puddings made with ale and rum and done up in white cloths, which retailed at £1.07½ ($4.17) the month that I was born. Some of these apparently stable *massifs* were more stable than others and I once saw and heard with indescribable delight a whole display of tins of Scotch shortbread avalanche to the ground, making a most satisfactory noise.

In the great vaulted hall, decorated with medieval scenes of the chase, and with metal racks for hanging the trophies of it, where Harrods's Fishmongers and Purveyors of Game and the assembled Butchers confronted one another across the central aisle, there were other mountainous displays of crabs, scallops, Aberdeen smokes, turbot and halibut, Surrey fowls and game in season on one side; and on the other, hecatombs of Angus Beef, South Down Lamb and Mutton.

The savannas were on the second floor, in Model Gowns, Model Coats and Model Costumes, endless expanses of carpet with here and there a solitary creation on a stand rising above it, like lone trees in a wilderness.

29

To me unutterably tedious were the unending, snowy-white wastes of the Linen Hall, coloured bed linen, coloured blankets, even coloured bath towels, except for the ends (headings) which were sometimes decorated with blue or red stripes, being – if not unknown – unthinkable at that time (coloured blankets, usually red, were for ambulances and hospitals). In it articles were on sale that not even my mother was tempted to buy: tablecloths eight yards long to fit tables that could seat two dozen guests, sheets and blankets ten feet wide, specially made to fit the big, old four-poster beds still apparently being slept in by some customers, in their moated granges.

Higher still, on the third floor, were what I regarded as the deserts of the Furniture Departments. It took something like ten minutes to get around these vast, and to me as uninteresting as the Linen Hall, expanses, in which the distances between the individual pieces were measured in yards rather than feet.

This 'Harrods's World' even had its own animal population in what the management called Livestock up on the second floor, what customers of my age group and most grown-ups called the zoo. In it the noise was deafening, what with macaws that could live for sixty years or so, Electus parrots in brilliant greens and reds and purples, according to sex, parrots that could speak – they had to pass a test to ensure that they did not use bad language – and other rare Asian birds, as well as puppies, kittens, guinea-pigs, mice, tortoises, armadillos and Malabar squirrels. I got my first mouse at Harrods.

But the greatest treat of all was a visit to the Book Department. I was not allowed to visit the Toy Department, except for my birthday, or at Christmas. In fact it was not very interesting except at Christmas time when it expanded for a month or two, then contracted again when the sales began in January, until the following November or December; and it was never as good in those days as Hamleys Toy Shop in Regent Street.

Although my mother refused to supply me with toys on demand on these journeys through Harrods (for that is what they were to me), she would always allow me to choose a book. The first book I can ever remember having, a Dean's Rag Book, printed on untearable linen, came from Harrods, although even then I found it difficult to think of something printed on linen (or whatever it was) as a book. Once I was in the Book Department it was very difficult to dislodge me, and it was only because I was actually being bought a book that I left it without tears, and to this day I find it almost impossible even to walk through this department en route elsewhere, without buying a book I didn't know I wanted.

Beyond the Book Department was the huge, reverberating, rather dimly lit Piano Department, where salesmen who dressed and looked like bank managers used to hover among the instruments, trying to put a brave face on it when I ran my fingers along the keys of their Bechstein Grands as we passed through, probably on our way to Gramophone Records, of which my mother, who loved dance music and dancing, had already amassed a large collection. Sometimes a visitor to the store who was also a pianist would take his seat at one of the grand pianos and this otherwise rather gloomy room would be filled with wonderful sounds.

It was from this department that there emanated, by way of Accounts, a bill made out to my father for one of these grand pianos, at a cost of something like £125 ($531) but expressed in guineas, which when it was finally sorted out was reduced to one of about £1.25 ($5.31) for a couple of visits by a piano tuner to Three Ther Mansions in order to tune our modest, upright Chappell, the grand piano having been charged to him in error. Until long after the Second World War, really until they installed a computer, Accounts had a dottiness about them that was sometimes, but not always, endearing; and until the computer was installed it was perfectly possible to order a pound or two of smoked salmon to be delivered from the Food Hall and not actually pay for it until three or more months later.

After seeing some or all of all this, for if my mother went to Harrods in the morning she would also spend part of the afternoon there, she would whisk me off to the Ladies' Retiring Room on the fourth floor where she freshened us both up before taking me to lunch in the Restaurant where, jacked up in a special infant's chair which elevated my nose and mouth above what would have been, sitting in an ordinary chair, the level of the table, I ate what at that time was my favourite meal, half portions of tomato soup, fried plaice and creamed potatoes.

A Traveller on Horseback

Christina Dodwell

It was time for me to go travelling again by horse. I knew the journey would be more fun in a wild part of the world, and what particularly attracted me were the remoter regions of Turkey and Iran.

It's odd how people try to put a woman off such ideas by saying it's too dangerous and she might be killed. My instinct told me that this was unlikely; in all the other journeys I've made the same warnings have been untrue. As for the threat of bandits or arrest by revolutionaries, I trusted in my common sense and doubted there would still be bandits nowadays.

Turkey's strategic position as a land-bridge spanning two continents has given it a colourful ten thousand years of surging and receding invasions. But it was surprisingly difficult to buy a good map. The Turkish ones had enlargements of western Turkey but the east was shown only in small scale and much of it looked empty. The lack of main roads would be no problem on horseback, however...

...Mount Ararat, I pondered which way to ride up it. We must assume that Noah was the first man to climb down Ararat. But the first to climb up it was a German called Dr Parrot who made the ascent in 1829. The easy approach from Doğubayazit didn't appeal to me since today most climbing groups go that way and it sounded crowded. When you've got a whole mountain, why follow the beaten track?

A south-east route would have taken me up on to the col between the great and small Ararats, but this alpine pastureland would be full of Kurdish *yailas*, and I had been told stories of a couple of American climbers who had everything stolen, including their boots.

The north and east faces of Ararat look into Russia and the area is prohibited to tourists, a shame because from there one can see up the abyss, a 3,000-metre chasm that splits the mountainside up to its summit massif, and it is overhung by 1,000 metres of glaciers. So Keyif and I would try a western approach. Once there was a village called Ahora and a monastery dedicated to St James on the north side of the mountain but both were destroyed by the massive earthquake of 1840 which threw the Araxes river out of its bed in the plain below. Today a new village stands nearby, and the north side has the added curiosity of a rocky outcrop shaped like the prow of a ship, which has often been mistaken for the Ark.

I liked the idea of looking for Noah's Ark. Soon after the 1840 earthquake there had been various sightings of the Ark, the first by a team of Turkish surveyors and workmen who went to check for danger of avalanches. They reported finding the front section of a large boat protruding from a glacier. Experts were sent to examine it and they climbed into some of the boat's well-preserved storage holds, but complete examination was not possible since most of it was still enclosed in ice.

In 1893 the highly respected Archdeacon of Babylon and Jerusalem, Dr Nouri, launched an expedition. He too found the Ark and announced that he had entered the bows and stern, although the central part was still icebound. He mentioned very thick hull timbers held together by 300-centimetre pegs. The archdeacon was an intelligent and educated man, speaking over ten languages, and a friend of the American President Roosevelt, and it seemed unlikely that his story was a hoax.

Other reports came from Russian pilots during the First World War; stories that were initially laughed at then checked out by senior officers, who agreed it was true, the Ark was still there. The Tsar authorized an army expedition. It returned with photographs, but these were lost during the Russian Revolution.

In the Second World War another Russian expedition claimed to have located the Ark, badly rotted by this time and in the process of submerging back into a glacier.

While I was riding through Turkey, an American had been applying for permission to dig for Noah's Ark. He believed he knew where it now lay and was coming armed with special electronic equipment. But at the last minute the Turkish authorities had rescinded his permit and decided to investigate his spot for themselves. I felt a little sorry for him. Personally I didn't expect to find the Ark, but that didn't stop me from looking.

The next morning dawned clear, and Keyif and I set out via the corn-merchant, where I strapped some extra barley in a sack behind the saddle, and saluted the gendarmes who had recovered my stolen goods. It took only ten minutes to leave town, Keyif was so fresh he raced along skittishly and shied at every vehicle on the road.

Once clear of the town we headed towards the west side of the mountain, aiming to run up between two parallel arms of lava. Before long the land underfoot became spongy and I could see reedbeds and marshland ahead so we detoured to the west and tried again. The morning sun was building up a hellish heat, yet high above were glaciers.

The slopes were extremely tricky, the giant lava flows were jagged with crevasses that Keyif could not cross, the land between lava tongues was boggy, much wetter than would be expected after rainfall, and it made me agree with the recent scientific theory that Mount Ararat contains a vast lake inside its bulk. People had warned me that water is a curious problem on Ararat because although there is a massive ice-cap there are very few springs or streams. And their length is short, they flow back into holes in the mountainside. A vast subterranean cavern is plausible when one considers the inner working of molten volcanic activity, and it ties in with the last eruption producing steam and gases instead of lava.

Reaching an area where the marsh had dried to a crazy-paving of crusty slabs I heaved a sigh of relief. Keyif was less sure, he didn't like the fissures between them and he was not at all keen to walk where I directed him. At first the crust supported his weight and we progressed quite far until suddenly it gave way.

The slabs cracked and dust exploded upwards. Keyif floundered, thrashing with his legs but was unable to find any firm foothold, and we were sinking fast. I was almost blinded with dust and shock; realising the dry bog was probably made of volcanic ash, possibly bottomless.

We had already sunk down over one metre, but Keyif had managed instinctively to turn around and was plunging desperately towards the point where we had entered. All I could do was cling on to his mane and shout encouragement.

That was the first of many dry and wet quagmires that we fell into over the next twenty-four hours while Mount Ararat lived up to its popular reputation as a mountain that does not wish to be climbed. Ancient nomads believed it was guarded by angels and forbidden to men. A lot of talk nowadays centres on its dangers, like the zone of snakes. But I would see for myself.

Keyif and I were battling into a strong headwind and I could feel rain drops coming from behind us. With luck the wind would push the rain away. We reached about 3,000 metres; I wondered how long it would be before Keyif began feeling the effects of the altitude.

This western side, even down on the plain, is almost uninhabited and uncultivated, there seems to be no water. Above us tall rocks reached up like spires. The eastern plain is more populated, with villages that bear names such as Nakhitchevan, meaning 'the place where Noah disembarked', and there is a site called Noah's burial place, and Ahora which means 'vine plantation'. Among the birds and beasts saved by the Ark, Noah also brought a collection of plants, and the vine was one of them.

The book of Genesis (chapter 9, verse 20) tells that Noah planted a vine after landing on Ararat. His son, Shem, took vines with him to the south-east and south-west. In fact, this geographical region is said to be the original home of the vine and, as I'd seen near Lake Van, it was an early centre for vine cultivation with sophisticated techniques of wine-making by 800 BC.

Despite the headwind, rain was now lashing down. As before, Keyif panicked at the crackle of my rainproof sheet and I had to fold it away. There was no point in seeking shelter since we were already soaked. I had noticed some *yailas*, but Keyif had spotted their horses and he began stamping and whinnying. That mare in Doğubayazit had scrambled his brains. Even the faintest horse-like shape in the distance made him prance with excitement.

The rain eased to drizzle and finally to wet mist. When I opened my saddlebags to put on dry clothes I discovered that rain had funnelled in through a hole in the plastic lining and everything was damp. The two most vital items were my sleeping bag, now useless, and my notebook, also useless because a biro doesn't write on wet paper. A pencil would have worked but I didn't have one. Weighing up my feelings about a cold wet bed against my mistrust of the Kurds here, I stopped overnight at a *yaila*. The women helped me to dry out my clothes on their dung-fuelled fire, and were as kind and hospitable as Kurds can be. Keyif was a bundle of energy, racing to and fro on his tether and roaring at the mares, he had no interest in food, water or sleep.

Dawn was misty, and when I went to collect Keyif he seemed to have no outline, just a grey blur in a grey fog. He was still prancing with energy, his mane streaming out and his nostrils steaming. A cold damp morning, I shivered uncomfortably and we got rather lost because mist shrouded the whole landscape; billowing and thinning, putting stark lines into soft focus. At our highest point I saw, looming blackly out of the opalescent blur, the tall prow-like shape of the Ark Rock. From this angle it certainly did look convincingly like a ship.

A shepherd I met said that the mist could stay for days. That was enough for me and I headed Keyif downhill. As we came down we reached the level where the clouds ended and beneath us was warm sunshine. Below that, the descent through lava spews grew continually hotter until around us was a volcanic bomb-field, scorching under a relentless sun.

I didn't mind about not reaching the summit. One cannot fail unless one sets out to succeed. Goals are like destinations, they don't always matter. Our journey was enough in itself.

The Stowaway

Julian Barnes

He was a large man, Noah – about the size of a gorilla, although there the resemblance ends. The flotilla's captain – he promoted himself to Admiral halfway through the Voyage – was an ugly old thing, both graceless in movement and indifferent to personal hygiene. He didn't even have the skill to grow his own hair except around his face; for the rest of his covering he relied on the skins of other species. Put him side by side with the gorilla and you will easily discern the superior creation: the one with graceful movement, rippling strength and an instinct for delousing. On the Ark we puzzled ceaselessly at the riddle of how God came to choose man as His protégé ahead of the more obvious candidates. He would have found most other species a lot more loyal. If He'd plumped for the gorilla, I doubt there'd have been half so much disobedience – probably no need to have had the Flood in the first place.

And the smell of the fellow... Wet fur growing on a species which takes pride in grooming is one thing; but a dank, salt-encrusted pelt hanging ungroomed from the neck of a negligent species to whom it doesn't belong is quite another matter. Even when the calmer times came, old Noah didn't seem to dry out (I am reporting what the birds said, and the birds could be trusted). He carried the damp and the storm around with him like some guilty memory or the promise of more bad weather...

It has to be said that Noah, rain or shine, wasn't much of a sailor. He was picked for his piety rather than his navigational skills. He wasn't any good in a storm, and he wasn't much better when the seas were calm. How would I be any judge? Again, I am reporting what the birds said – the birds that can stay in the air for weeks at a time, the birds that can find their way from one end of the planet to the other by navigational systems as elaborate as any invented by your species. And the *birds* said

Noah didn't know what he was doing – he was all bluster and prayer. It wasn't difficult, what he had to do, was it? During the tempest he had to survive by running from the fiercest part of the storm; and during calm weather he had to ensure we didn't drift so far from our original map-reference that we came to rest in some uninhabitable Sahara. The best that can be said for Noah is that he survived the storm (though he hardly needed to worry about reefs and coastlines, which made things easier), and that when the waters finally subsided we didn't find ourselves by mistake in the middle of some great ocean. If we'd done that, there's no knowing how long we'd have been at sea.

Of course, the birds offered to put their expertise at Noah's disposal; but he was too proud. He gave them a few simple reconnaissance tasks – looking out for whirlpools and tornadoes – while disdaining their proper skills. He also sent a number of species to their deaths by asking them to go aloft in terrible weather when they weren't properly equipped to do so. When Noah despatched the warbling goose into a Force Nine gale (the bird did, it's true, have an irritating cry, especially if you were trying to sleep), the stormy petrel actually volunteered to take its place. But the offer was spurned – and that was the end of the warbling goose . . .

... When the Ark landed on the mountaintop (it was more complicated than that, of course, but we'll let details pass), Noah sent out a raven and a dove to see if the waters had retreated from the face of the earth. Now, in the version that has come down to you, the raven has a very small part; it merely flutters hither and thither, to little avail, you are led to conclude. The dove's three journeys, on the other hand, are made a matter of heroism. We weep when she finds no rest for the sole of her foot; we rejoice when she returns to the Ark with an olive leaf. You have elevated this bird, I understand, into something of symbolic value. So let me just point this out: the raven always maintained that *he* found the olive tree; that *he* brought a leaf from it back to the Ark; but that Noah decided it was 'more appropriate' to say that the dove had discovered it. Personally, I always believed the raven, who apart from anything else was much stronger in the air than the dove; and it would have been just like Noah (modelling himself on that God of his again) to stir up a dispute among the animals. Noah had it put about that the raven, instead of returning as soon as possible with evidence of dry land, had been malingering, and had been spotted (by whose eye? not even the upwardly mobile dove would have demeaned herself with such a slander) gourmandising on carrion. The raven, I need hardly add, felt hurt and betrayed at this instant rewriting of history, and it is said – by those with a better ear than mine – that you can hear the sad croak of dissatisfaction in his voice to this day. The dove, by contrast, began sounding unbearably smug from the moment we disembarked. She could already envisage herself on postage stamps and letterheads.

Before the ramps were lowered, 'the Admiral' addressed the beasts on his Ark, and his words were relayed to those of us on other ships. He thanked us for our co-operation, he apologized for the occasional sparseness of rations, and he promised that since we had all kept our side of the bargain, he was going to get the best *quid pro quo* out of God in the forthcoming negotiations. Some of us laughed a little doubtingly at that: we remembered the keel-hauling of the ass, the loss of the hospital ship, the exterminatory policy with cross-breeds, the death of the unicorn ...It was evident to us that if Noah was coming on all Mister Nice Guy, it was because he sensed what any clear-thinking animal would do the moment it placed its foot on dry land: make for the forests and the hills. He was obviously trying to soft-soap us into staying close to New Noah's Palace, whose construction he chose to announce at the same time. Amenities here would include free water for the animals and extra feed during harsh winters. He was obviously scared that the meat diet he'd got used to on the Ark would be taken away from him as fast as its two, four or however many legs could carry it, and that the Noah family would be back on berries and nuts once again. Amazingly, some of the beasts thought Noah's offer a fair one: after all, they argued, he can't eat all of us, he'll probably just cull the old and the sick. So some of them – not the cleverest ones, it has to be said – stayed around waiting for the Palace to be built and the water to flow like wine. The pigs, the cattle, the sheep, some of the stupider goats, the chickens . . . We warned them, or at least we tried. We used to mutter derisively, 'Braised or boiled?' but to no avail. As I say, they weren't very bright, and were probably their gaol, and their gaoler. What happened over the next few generations was quite predictable: they became shadows of their former selves. The pigs and sheep you see walking around today are zombies compared to their effervescent ancestors on the Ark. They've had the stuffing knocked out of them. And some of them, like the turkey, have to endure the further indignity of having the stuffing put back into them – before they are braised or boiled...

...Getting off the Ark, I think I told you, wasn't much easier than getting on. There had, alas, been a certain amount of ratting by some of the chosen species, so there was no question of Noah simply flinging down the ramps and crying 'Happy land'. Every animal had to put up with a strict body-search before being released; some were even doused in tubs of water which smelt of tar. Several female beasts complained of having to undergo internal examination by Shem. Quite a few stowaways were discovered: some of the more conspicuous beetles, a few rats who had unwisely gorged themselves during the Voyage and got too fat, even a snake or two. We got off – I don't suppose it need be a secret any longer – in the hollowed tip of a ram's horn. It was a big, surly, subversive animal, whose friendship we had deliberately cultivated for the last three years at sea. It had no respect for Noah, and was only too happy to help outsmart him after the Landing.

When the seven of us climbed out of that ram's horn, we were euphoric. We had survived. We had stowed away, survived and escaped – all without entering into any fishy covenants with either God or Noah. We had done it by ourselves. We felt ennobled as a species. That might strike you as comic, but we did: we felt ennobled. That Voyage taught us a lot of things, you see, and the main thing was this: that man is a very unevolved species compared to the animals. We don't deny, of course, your cleverness, your considerable potential. But you are, as yet, at an early stage of your development. We, for instance, are always ourselves: that is what it means to be evolved. We are what we are, and we know what that is. You don't expect a cat suddenly to start barking, do you, or a pig to start lowing? But this is what, in a manner of speaking, those of us who made the Voyage on the

Ark learned to expect from your species. One moment you bark, one moment you mew; one moment you wish to be wild, one moment you wish to be tame. We knew where we were with Noah only in this one respect: that we never knew where we were with him.

A Lady's Life in the Rocky Mountains

Isabella Bird

With her small support team, Victorian explorer, Isabella Bird, prepares to make the hazardous ascent of one of the highest peaks in America's Rocky Mountains . . .

As we crept from the lodge round a horn of rock, I beheld what made me perfectly sick and dizzy to look at – the terminal Peak itself – a smooth, cracked face or wall of pink granite, as nearly perpendicular as anything could well be up which it was possible to climb, well deserving the name of the 'American Matterhorn'.

Scaling, not climbing, is the correct term for this last ascent. It took one hour to accomplish 500 feet, pausing for breath every minute or two. The only foothold was in narrow cracks or on minute projections on the granite. To get a toe in these cracks, or here and there on a scarcely obvious projection, while crawling on hands and knees, all the while tortured with thirst and gasping and struggling for breath, this was the climb; but at last the Peak was won. A grand, well-defined mountain-top it is, a nearly level acre of boulders, with precipitous sides all round, the one we came up being the only accessible one.

It was not possible to remain long. One of the young men was seriously alarmed by bleeding from the lungs, and the intense dryness of the day and the rarefaction of the air, at a height of nearly 15,000 feet, made respiration very painful. There is always water on the Peak, but it was frozen as hard as a rock, and the sucking of ice and snow increases thirst. We all suffered severely from the want of water, and the gasping for breath made our mouths and tongues so dry that articulation was difficult, and the speech of all unnatural.

From the summit were seen in unrivalled combination all the views which had rejoiced our eyes during the ascent. It was something at last to stand upon the storm-rent crown of this lonely sentinel of the Rocky Range, on one of the mightiest of the vertebræ of the backbone of the North American continent, and to see the waters start for both oceans. Uplifted above love and hate and storms of passion, calm amidst the eternal silences, fanned by zephyrs and bathed in living blue, peace rested for that one bright day on the Peak, as if it were some region:

> Where falls not rain, or hail, or any snow,
> Or ever wind blows loudly.

We placed our names, with the date of ascent, in a tin within a crevice, and descended to the Ledge, sitting on the smooth granite, getting our feet into cracks and against projections, and letting ourselves down by our hands, 'Jim' going before me, so that I might steady my feet against his powerful shoulders. I was no longer giddy, and faced the precipice of 3500 feet without a shiver. Repassing the Ledge and Lift, we accomplished the descent through 1500 feet of ice and snow, with many falls and bruises, but no worse mishap, and there separated, the young men taking the steepest but most direct way to the Notch, with the intention of getting ready for the march home, and 'Jim' and I taking what he thought the safer route for me – a descent over boulders for 2000 feet, and then a tremendous ascent to the 'Notch'. I had various falls, and once hung by my frock, which caught on a rock, and 'Jim' severed it with his hunting-knife, upon which I fell into a crevice full of soft snow. We were driven lower down the mountains than he had intended by impassable tracts of ice, and the ascent was tremendous. For the last 200 feet the boulders were of enormous size, and the steepness fearful. Sometimes I drew myself up on hands and knees, sometimes crawled; sometimes 'Jim' pulled me up by my arms or a lariat, and sometimes I stood on his shoulders, or he made steps for me of his feet and hands, but at six we stood on the Notch in the splendour of the sinking sun, all colour deepening, all peaks glorifying, all shadows purpling, all peril past.

'Jim' had parted with his *brusquerie* when we parted from the students, and was gentle and considerate beyond anything, though I knew that he must be grievously disappointed, both in my courage and strength. Water was an object of earnest desire. My tongue rattled in my mouth, and I could hardly articulate. It is good for one's sympathies to have for once a severe experience of thirst. Truly, there was:

> Water, water everywhere,
> But not a drop to drink.

Three times its apparent gleam deceived even the mountaineer's practised eye, but we found only a foot of 'glare ice'. At last, in a deep hole, he succeeded in breaking the ice, and by putting one's arm far down one could scoop up a little water in one's hand, but it was tormentingly insufficient. With great difficulty and much assistance I recrossed the 'Lava Beds', was carried to the horse and lifted upon him, and when we reached the camping ground I was lifted off him, and laid on the ground wrapped up in blankets, a humiliating termination of a great exploit. The horses were saddled, and the young men were all ready to start, but 'Jim' quietly said, 'Now, gentlemen, I want a good night's rest, and we shan't stir from here to-night.' I believe they were really glad to have it so, as one of them was quite 'finished'. I retired to my arbour, wrapped myself in a roll of blankets, and was soon asleep. When I woke, the moon was high shining through the silvery branches, whitening the bald Peak above, glittering on the great abyss of snow behind, and pine logs were blazing like a bonfire in the cold still air. My feet were so icy cold that I could not sleep again, and getting some blankets to sit in, and making a roll of them for my back, I sat for two hours by the camp fire. It was weird and gloriously beautiful. The students were asleep not far off in their blankets with their feet towards the fire. 'Ring' lay on one side of me with his fine head on my arm, and his master sat smoking, with the fire lighting up the handsome side of his face, and except for the tones of our voices, and an occasional crackle and splutter as a pine knot blazed up, there was no sound on the mountain side. The beloved stars of my far-off home were overhead, the Plough and Pole Star, with their steady light; the glittering Pleiades, looking larger than I ever saw them, and 'Orion's studded belt' shining gloriously. Once only some wild animals prowled near the camp, when 'Ring,' with one bound, disappeared from my side; and the horses, which were picketed by the stream, broke their lariats, stampeded, and came rushing wildly towards the fire, and it was fully half an hour before they were caught and quiet was restored. 'Jim', or Mr Nugent, as I always scrupulously called him, told stories of his early youth, and of a great sorrow which had led him to embark on a lawless and desperate life. His voice trembled, and tears rolled down his cheek. Was it semi-conscious acting, I wondered, or was his dark soul really stirred to its depths by the silence, the beauty, and the memories of youth?

We reached Estes Park at noon of the following day. A more successful ascent of the Peak was never made, and I would not now exchange my memories of its perfect beauty and extraordinary sublimity for any other experience of mountaineering in any part of the world. Yesterday snow fell on the summit, and it will be inaccessible for eight months to come.

I. L. B.

All on the Bornean Shore

Charles Hose

Examining the wildlife of Borneo in the 1920s, explorer Charles Hose, describes the exotic creatures he sees along the shores close to camp...

Glancing around from our camping ground, one sees a number of long palm-poles sticking up out of the water. These are the remains of houses which have long since disappeared. If one taps one of these poles two or three small bats are sure to fly out, for the pith centre has long ago been destroyed and the hollow pole provides the creatures with a home where they can remain in peace and darkness during the daytime.

The sea now being perfectly calm, native fishermen can be seen farther along the beach engaged in catching fish with a drag-net. On approaching them we see that one end of the net is carried out to sea by some of the party, who wade in to their necks, and are just able to hold on to the net while those in a boat play it out in a half circle until the entire net has run out. Then, moving round, they complete the whole circle, and, closing in at either end, the two parties with their united effort drag the net ashore.

Anxious to see what sort of catch they have made, we move closer, and in the pocket in the centre of the net we find many beautiful edible fish, such as bass, horse-mackerel (*Trachurus*), walking-fish (*Antennarius*), mingled with sting-ray (*Trygon*), small sharks, and various kinds of cat-fish. Among them were one or two horrid, poisonous, spiny little fish such as the sea dragon (*Pegasus draco*), the horned trunk-fish or *Ostracion cornutus*, and *Tetrodon* or Balloon-fish, a curious creature with many sharp spikes which often cause great pain to the natives if their bare feet come into contact with them in the water. The

Pipe-fish, also called needle-fish (*Syngnathus*), is common along the shores, and may be included in the catch. The flesh of certain species of Plotosus (the Semilang of the Malays) has a good flavour, but it is rather indigestible; a very fine glue is made from its swimming blades which looks like a sort of isinglass. This fish is of a greenish colour, and much eaten by other fish; sometimes it reaches a considerable size – specimens seven feet long and weighing as much as sixty pounds have been captured. The horned trunk-fish (*Ostracion cornutus*) is a curious-looking creature which is constantly brought up in the fishing nets. They are called Pectognathi because their jaws are coalescent. The family of Trunk-fishes are known by the curious structure of their external surface, composed of a series of hard scales forming a continuous bony armour. The body is either three or four-sided, and covered with this solid coat of mail in which the scales or plates are six-sided, and this armour is pierced with holes through which protrude the mouth, tail, and fins. The entire interior structure is modified in accordance with this external, inflexible cuirass. If we compare the general form of this creature with that of certain reptiles, the analogy between the Trunk-fish and the Tortoise is too close to escape observation. None of these fish are in demand as articles of food, and, generally speaking, are supposed to have a poisonous effect.

Here also we find the *Hippocampus*, the little 'sea-horse' or 'sea-dragon' common in many European and tropical seas, and sometimes found on the British coast. These fishes have but one dorsal fin, set far back, and capable of being moved in a marvellously swift fashion which reminds one of a screw-propeller, and evidently answers a similar purpose. The tail of the sea-horse, stiff as it appears to be in dried specimens, is, during the life of the creature, almost as flexible as an elephant's trunk, and is employed as a prehensile organ to anchor the sea-horse to weeds or other fixed objects. Some of these sea-horses can be seen in the new Aquarium at the Zoological Gardens in Regent's Park, Sir Peter Chalmers Mitchell having brought the original supply from the Mediterranean by aeroplane...

...Perhaps the most curious of this collection is the *Buntal* or Balloon-fish, which, as soon as it is landed, or comes into shallow water, begins sucking in air with strange noises until its skin is completely blown out. This *Tetrodon* or four-toothed fish, normally some six inches long, but about the size of a goose's egg when inflated, and resembling a gigantic horse-chestnut, has quite an array of soft spiny points on its skin which project in every direction when it is filled with air and blown out. Both jaws are divided in the middle, giving the fish the appearance of possessing four sets of teeth, two above and two below – hence its name *Tetrodon*. When the balloon-fish is inflated, it turns on its back, and, if in the shallows, floats belly uppermost. Not until the air has once more escaped can it immerse itself below the surface. There is one species beautifully marked with golden stripes. The balloon-fish is not considered fit for food by the natives of Borneo, and, for this reason, when it is caught in the nets – inflated to its fullest extent and being quite useless – they stamp violently upon it in disgust, causing a devastating report like a boy bursting a paper bag.

Into the Heart of Borneo

Redmond O'Hanlon

Travelling through Borneo, Redmond O'Hanlon, James Fenton and their team experience some uncomfortable moments as they investigate the region's wildlife . . .

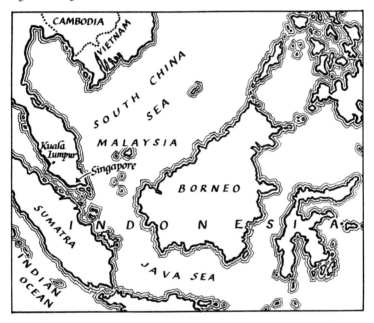

James appeared, closely followed by Inghai and Leon. James looked very hot. He sat on the tree trunk next to Dana, held his head in his hand – and then bounded up with a yell. There was a leech on his left arm. He pulled it off with his right hand, but the leech looped over and sank its mouthparts into his palm. James began to dance, wriggling convulsively. He made a curious yelping sound. The Iban lay down, and laughed. James pulled the leech out of his right palm with his left hand. The brown-black, tough, rubbery, segmented, inch-long Common ground leech, *Haemadipsa zeylanica*, then twisted over and began to take a drink at the base of James's thumb.

'Shit!' said James.

At this point, Leon obviously decided that the two had got to know each other well enough.

'Ah, my best friend,' he said to James, as he pulled the leech out, rubbed it on a tree and cut it in half with his parang, 'why you come so far to suffer so? Eh?'

James sat down, trembling a bit, and pulled out a cigarette.

'For bully beef,' said Dana suddenly, the English of his army days unexpectedly coming back to him. 'For Badas bully beef.'

'I don't know about that, but I certainly feel I'm being bullied,' said James. 'There is *absolutely no need* to treat this as an endurance test. From now on, I shall be in second place and we will all be sensible about it.'

James, I decided, was an admirable man in every way, having just saved us from death by heart attack, or an all-in melting of the arteries.

'Okay,' I said, shrugging my shoulders as if I had actually been about to suggest that we take the next stage at a sprint. 'It's all the same to me.'

'Jams, my very best friend,' said Leon, 'you not be angries. Our Tuai Rumah – he always walk fast. He want to tell us he not an old man. He want to tell us he the strongest in the longhouse.'

I looked at my legs. And then I looked again. They were undulating with leeches. In fact James's leech suddenly seemed much less of a joke. They were edging up my trousers, looping up towards my knees with alternate placements of their anterior and posterior suckers, seeming, with each rear attachment, to wave their front ends in the air and take a sniff. They were all over my boots, too, and three particularly brave individuals were trying to make their way in via the air-holes. There were more on the way – in fact they were moving towards us across the jungle floor from every angle, their damp brown bodies half-camouflaged against the rotting leaves.

'Oh God,' said James, '*they are really pleased to see us.*'

The Iban were also suffering, and we spent the next few minutes pulling leeches off our persons and wiping them on the trees. The bite of *Haemadipsa zeylanica* is painless (although that of the Borneo tiger-leech is pungent), containing an anaesthetic in its saliva as well as an anti-coagulant, but nonetheless it was unpleasant to watch them fill with blood at great speed, distending, becoming globular and wobbly.

Now that I had become accustomed to leech-spotting I discovered that they were rearing up and sniffing at us from the trees, too, from leaves and creepers at face height. We covered ourselves with Autan jelly, socks and trousers, chests, arms and neck. Dana, Leon and Inghai put on their best (and only) pairs of long trousers, and I lent them pairs of socks (they were desperate). I took the opportunity to sidle off behind a bush and fill my boots and y-fronts with handfuls of zinc powder. Sitting down again, I was pleased to see that chemical warfare works: the leeches looped and flowed towards me and then stopped, in mid-sniff, as disgusted by me as I was by them. They waved their heads about, thought a bit, decided that they really were revolted, and reversed.

We set off at a more gentlemanly pace, a slow climb and descent which gave us time to drink one bottleful of water at every third gully from the clear tumbling streams, refill it, drop in two water-purifying pills, and drink the second bottle at the next pause, repeating the process. Inspecting every tiny rock-pool in which I submerged my flask, I was grateful for Audy and Harrison's warning: there was invariably a Thread leech or two stretching itself towards my hand from the rounded tops of adjacent stones, looking, between each bunching movement, exactly like a pale length of cotton thread. It would have been annoying to have gulped one in, to have it swelling in the throat or setting off for a leisurely peek down the windpipe.

In the Jungle

Annie Dillard

Like any out-of-the-way place, the Napo River in the Ecua-
dorian jungle seems real enough when you are there, even
central. Out of the way of *what?* I was sitting on a stump at the
edge of a bankside palm-thatch village, in the middle of the
night, on the headwaters of the Amazon. Out of the way of
human life, tenderness, or the glance of heaven?

A nightjar in deep-leaved shadow called three long notes, and
hushed. The men with me talked softly in clumps: three North
Americans, four Ecuadorians who were showing us the jungle.
We were holding cool drinks and idly watching a hand-sized
tarantula seize moths that came to the lone bulb on the generator
shed beside us.

It was February, the middle of summer. Green fireflies
spattered lights across the air and illumined for seconds, now
here, now there, the pale trunks of enormous, solitary trees.
Beneath us the brown Napo River was rising, in all silence; it
coiled up the sandy bank and tangled its foam in vines that
trailed from the forest and roots that looped the shore.

Each breath of night smelled sweet, more moistened and
sweet than any kitchen, or garden, or cradle. Each star in Orion
seemed to tremble and stir with my breath. All at once, in the
thatch house across the clearing behind us, one of the village's
Jesuit priests began playing an alto recorder, playing a wordless
song, lyric, in a minor key, that twined over the village clearing,
that caught in the big trees' canopies, muted our talk on the
bankside, and wandered over the river, dissolving downstream.

This will do, I thought. This will do, for a weekend, or a
season, for a home.

Later that night I loosed my hair from its braids and combed it smooth – not for myself, but so the village girls could play with it in the morning.

We had disembarked at the village that afternoon, and I had slumped on some shaded steps, wishing I knew some Spanish or some Quechua so I could speak with the ring of little girls who were alternately staring at me and smiling at their toes. I spoke anyway, and fooled with my hair, which they were obviously dying to get their hands on, and laughed, and soon they were all braiding my hair, all five of them, all fifty fingers, all my hair, even my bangs. And then they took it apart and did it again, laughing, and teaching me Spanish nouns, and meeting my eyes and each other's with open delight, while their small brothers in blue jeans climbed down from the trees and began kicking a volleyball around with one of the North American men.

Now, as I combed my hair in the little tent, another of the men, a free-lance writer from Manhattan, was talking quietly. He was telling us the tale of his life, describing his work in Hollywood, his apartment in Manhattan, his house in Paris . . . 'It makes me wonder,' he said, 'what I'm doing in a tent under a tree in the village of Pompeya, on the Napo River, in the jungle of Ecuador.' After a pause he added, 'It makes me wonder why I'm going *back*.'

The point of going somewhere like the Napo River in Ecuador is not to see the most spectacular anything. It is simply to see what is there. We are here on the planet only once, and might as well get a feel for the place. We might as well get a feel for the fringes and hollows in which life is lived, for the Amazon basin, which covers half a continent, and for the life that – there, like anywhere else – is always and necessarily lived in detail: on the tributaries, in the riverside villages, sucking this particular white fleshed guava in this particular pattern of shade.

What is there is interesting. The Napo River itself is wide (I mean wider than the Mississippi at Davenport) and brown, opaque, and smeared with floating foam and logs and branches from the jungle. White egrets hunch on shoreline deadfalls and parrots in flocks dart in and out of the light. Under the water in the river, unseen, are anacondas – which are reputed to take a few village toddlers every year – and water boas, sting-rays, crocodiles, manatees, and sweet-meated fish.

Low water bares grey strips of sandbar on which the natives build tiny palm-thatch shelters, arched, the size of pup tents, for overnight fishing trips. You see these extraordinarily clean people (who bathe twice a day in the river, and whose straight black hair is always freshly washed) paddling down the river in dugout canoes, hugging the banks.

Some of the Indians of this region, earlier in the century, used to sleep naked in hammocks. The nights are cold. Gordon MacCreach, an American explorer in these Amazon tributaries, reported that he was startled to hear the Indians get up at three in the morning. He was even more startled, night after night, to hear them walk down to the river slowly, half asleep, and bathe in the water. Only later did he learn what they were doing: they were getting warm. The cold woke them; they warmed their skins in the river, which was always ninety degrees; then they returned to their hammocks and slept through the rest of the night.

The riverbanks are low, and from the river you see an unbroken wall of dark forest in every direction, from the Andes to the Atlantic. You get a taste for looking at trees: trees hung with the swinging nests of yellow troupials, trees from which ant nests the size of grain sacks hang like black goiters, trees from which seven-coloured tanagers flutter, coral trees, teak, balsa and breadfruit, enormous emergent silk-cotton trees, and the pale-barked *samona* palms.

When you are inside the jungle, away from the river, the trees vault out of sight. It is hard to remember to look up the long trunks and see the fans, strips, fronds, and sprays of glossy leaves. Inside the jungle you are more likely to notice the snarl of climbers and creepers round the trees' boles, the flowering bromeliads and epiphytes in every bough's crook, and the fantastic silk-cotton tree trunks thirty or forty feet across, trunks buttressed in flanges of wood whose curves can make three high walls of a room – a shady, loamy-aired room where you would gladly live, or die. Butterflies, iridescent blue, striped, or clear-winged, thread the jungle paths at eye level. And at your feet is a swath of ants bearing triangular bits of green leaf. The ants with their leaves look like a wide fleet of sailing dinghies – but they don't quit. In either direction they wobble over the jungle floor as far as the eye can see. I followed them off the path as far as I dared, and never saw an end to ants or to those luffing chips of green they bore.

Unseen in the jungle, but present, are tapirs, jaguars, many species of snake and lizard, ocelots, armadillos, marmosets, howler monkeys, toucans and macaws and a hundred other birds, deer, bats, peccaries, capybaras, agoutis, and sloths. Also present in this jungle, but variously distant, are Texaco derricks and pipelines, and some of the wildest Indians in the world, blowgun-using Indians, who killed missionaries in 1956 and ate them.

Long lakes shine in the jungle. We travelled one of these in dugout canoes, canoes with two inches of freeboard, canoes paddled with machete-hewn oars chopped from buttresses of silk-cotton trees, or poled in the shallows with peeled cane or bamboo. Our part-Indian guide had cleared the path to the lake the day before; when we walked the path we saw where he had impaled the lopped head of a boa, open-mouthed, on a pointed stick by the canoes, for decoration.

This lake was wonderful. Herons, egrets, and ibises plodded the sawgrass shores, kingfishers and cuckoos clattered from sunlight to shade, great turkey-like birds fussed in dead branches, and hawks lolled overhead. There was all the time in the world. A turtle slid into the water. The boy in the bow of my canoe slapped stones at birds with a simple sling, a rubber thong and leather pad. He aimed brilliantly at moving targets, always, and always missed; the birds were out of range. He stuffed his sling back in his shirt. I looked around.

The lake and river waters are as opaque as rain-forest leaves; they are veils, blinds, painted screens. You see things only by their effects. I saw the shoreline water roll and the sawgrass heave about a thrashing *paichi*, an enormous black fish of these waters; one had been caught the previous week weighing 430 pounds. Piranha fish live in the lakes, and electric eels. I dangled my fingers in the water, figuring it would be worth it.

We would eat chicken that night in the village, and rice, yucca, onions, beets, and heaps of fruit. The sun would ring down, pulling darkness after it like a curtain. Twilight is short, and the unseen birds of twilight wistful, uncanny, catching the heart. The two nuns in their dazzling white habits – the beautiful-boned young nun and the warm-faced old – would glide to the open cane-and-thatch schoolroom in darkness, and start the children singing. The children would sing in piping Spanish, high-pitched and pure; they would sing 'Nearer My God to Thee' in Quechua, very fast. (To reciprocate, we sang for them 'Old MacDonald Had a Farm'; I thought they might recognize the animal sounds. Of course they thought we were out of our minds.) As the children became excited by their own singing, they left their log benches and swarmed around the nuns, hopping, smiling at us, everyone smiling, the nuns' faces bursting in their cowls, and the clear-voiced children still singing, and the palm-leafed roofing stirred.

The Napo River: it is not out of the way. It is in the way, catching sunlight the way a cup catches poured water; it is a bowl of sweet air, a basin of greenness, and of grace, and, it would seem, of peace.

Travellers

Tracks

Robyn Davidson

Robyn Davidson fulfils a strange ambition: to cross the Australian
Outback with camels. Here she arrives in Alice Springs where her
journey begins . . .

I arrived in the Alice at five a.m. with a dog, six dollars and a
small suitcase full of inappropriate clothes. 'Bring a cardigan for
the evenings,' the brochure said. A freezing wind whipped grit
down the platform and I stood shivering, holding warm dog
flesh, and wondering what foolishness had brought me to this
eerie, empty train-station in the centre of nowhere. I turned
against the wind, and saw the line of mountains at the edge of
town.

There are some moments in life that are like pivots around
which your existence turns – small intuitive flashes, when you
know you have done something correct for a change, when you
think you are on the right track. I watched a pale dawn streak the
cliffs with Day-glo and realized this was one of them. It was a
moment of pure, uncomplicated confidence – and lasted about
ten seconds...

...The lunatic idea was, basically, to get myself the requisite
number of wild camels from the bush and train them to carry my
gear, then walk into and about the central desert area. I knew
that there were feral camels aplenty in this country. They had
been imported in the 1850s along with their Afghani and North
Indian owners, to open up the inaccessible areas, to transport
food, and to help build the telegraph system and railways that
would eventually cause their economic demise. When this

happened, those Afghans had let their camels go, heartbroken, and tried to find other work. They were specialists and it wasn't easy. They didn't have much luck with government support either. Their camels, however, had found easy street – it was perfect country for them and they grew and prospered, so that now there are approximately ten thousand roaming the free country and making a nuisance of themselves on cattle properties, getting shot at, and, according to some ecologists, endangering some plant species for which they have a particular fancy. Their only natural enemy is man, they are virtually free of disease, and Australian camels are now rated as some of the best in the world...

...All I remember of that first day alone was a feeling of release; a sustained, buoyant confidence as I strolled along, Bub's nose-line in my sweaty palm, the camels in a well-behaved line behind me and Goliath bringing up the rear. The muffled tinkling of their bells, the soft crunching of my feet in the sand and the faint twittering of the wood-swallows were the only sounds. The desert was otherwise still.

I had decided to follow an abandoned track that would eventually meet up with the main Areyonga road. Now, the definition of a track in Australia is a mark made across the landscape by the repeated passage of a vehicle or, if you are very lucky, initially by a bulldozer. These tracks vary in quality from a corrugated, bull-dust-covered, well-defined and well-used road to something which you can barely discern by climbing a hill and squinting in the general direction you think the said track may go. Sometimes you can see where a track is by the tell-tale blossoms of wildflowers. Those along the track will either be growing more thickly or be of a different type. Sometimes, you may be able to follow the trail by searching for the ridge left aeons ago by a bulldozer. The track may wind around or over hills and ridges and rocky outcroppings, straight into sand-dunes, get swallowed up by sandy creek-beds, get totally lost in stony creek-beds, or fray into a maze of animal pads. Following tracks is most often easy, sometimes frustrating, and occasionally downright terrifying.

When you are in cattle or sheep station country, the following of tracks can be especially puzzling, mainly because one always assumes that a track will lead somewhere. This is not necessarily so since station people just don't think like that. Also there is the problem of choice. When you are presented with half a dozen tracks all leading off in the general direction you want to go, all used within the last year, and none of them marked on the map, which one do you choose? If you choose the wrong one it may simply stop five miles ahead, so that you have to back-track, having lost half a day's travel. Or it may lead you to an abandoned, waterless windmill and bore, or slap-bang into a new fence-line, which, if followed, will begin leading you in exactly the opposite direction to where you thought you wanted to go, only now you're not quite sure because you've made so many turnings and weavings that you are beginning to lose confidence in your sense of direction. Or it might lead you to a gate made by some jackaroo who thought he was Charles Atlas and which you haven't got a hope in hell of opening, or if you can open it without suffering a rupture, then closing it is impossible without using the camels as a winch, which takes half an hour to do and you're already hot and bothered and dusty and all you really want in life is to get to the next watering place and have an aspirin and a cup of tea and a good lie down.

This is complicated further by the fact that whoever those people are who fly in planes and make maps of the area, they need glasses; or perhaps were drunk at the time; or perhaps just felt like breaking free of departmental rulings and added a few bits and pieces of imaginative topography, or even, in some cases, rubbed out a few features in a fit of solitary anarchic vice. One expects maps to be always but always 100 per cent correct, and most of the time they are. It's those other times that can set you into a real panic. Make you doubt even your own senses. Make you think that perhaps that sand-ridge you swore you sat on back there was a mirage. Make you entertain the notion that you are sun-struck. Make you gulp once or twice and titter nervously.

However, that first day held none of these problems. If the track petered out into dust bowls with drinking spots in the middle of them, it was relatively easy to find where it continued on the other side. The camels were going well and behaving like lambs. Life was good. The country I was travelling through held my undivided attention with its diversity. This particular area had had three bumper seasons in succession and was carpeted in green and dotted with white, yellow, red, blue wildflowers. Then I would find myself in a creek-bed where tall gums and delicate acacias cast deep cool shadow. And birds. Everywhere birds. Black cockatoos, sulphur-cresteds, swallows, Major-Mitchells, willy-wagtails, quarrian, kestrels, budgerigar flocks, bronze-wings, finches. And there were kunga-berries and various solanums and mulga apples and eucalyptus manna to eat as I walked along. This searching for and picking wild food is one of the most pleasant, calming pastimes I know. Contrary to popular belief, the desert is bountiful and teeming with life in the good seasons. It is like a vast untended communal garden, the closest thing to earthly paradise I can imagine. Mind you, I wouldn't want to have to survive on bush-tucker during the drought. And even in the good season, I admit I would prefer my diet to be supplemented by the occasional tin of sardines, and a frequent cup of sweet billy tea...

...I was a little nervous my first night out. Not because I was frightened of the dark (the desert is benign and beautiful at night, and except for the eight-inch-long, pink millipedes that sleep under the bottom of the swag and may wish to bite you when you roll it up at dawn, or the careless straying of a scorpion under your sleep-twitching hand, or the lonely slithering of a Joe Blake who may want to cuddle up and get warm under the bedclothes then fang you to death when you wake up, there is not much to worry about) but because I wondered if I would ever see the camels again. I hobbled them out at dusk, unclogged their bells and tied little Goliath to a tree. Would it work, I asked myself? The answer came back, 'She'll be right, mate,' the closest thing to a Zen statement to come out of Australia, and one I used frequently in the months ahead.

The process of unloading had been infinitely easier than putting the stuff on. It only took an hour. Then there was wood to be gathered, a fire and lamp to be lit, camels to be checked on, cooking utensils, food and cassette player to be got out, Diggity to be fed, camels to be checked on, food to be cooked and camels to be checked on. They were munching their heads off happily enough. Except Goliath. He was yelling piggishly for his mother, who, thank god, was taking no notice whatsoever.

I think I cooked a freeze-dried dish that night. A vastly overrated cardboard-like substitute for edible food. The fruit was OK, you could eat that straight like biscuit, but the meat and vegetable dishes were tasteless soggy tack. I fed all my packets to the camels later on, and stuck with what was to be my staple diet: brown rice, lentils, garlic, curry, oil, pancakes made with all manner of cereals and coconut and dried egg, various root vegetables cooked in the coals, cocoa, tea, sugar, honey, powdered milk, and every now and then, the ultimate in luxury, a can of sardines, some pepperoni and Kraft cheese, a tin of fruit, and an orange or lemon. I supplemented this with vitamin pills, various wild foods, and the occasional rabbit. Far from being deficient, this diet made me so healthy, I felt like a cast-iron amazon; cuts and gashes vanished in a day, I could see almost as well at night as I could in sunlight, and I grew muscles on my shit.

After that first lack-lustre meal, I built the fire up, checked again on the camels, and put my Pitjantjara learning tapes into the cassette. *Nyuntu palya nyinanyi. Uwa, palyarna, palu nyuntu*, I mumbled repeatedly at the night sky now thick and gorgeous with billions of stars. There was no moon that night...

...But wouldn't it be my luck that on the third day, when I was still a puppy, a cub-scout in the ways of the bush, and still believing blindly that all maps were infallible and certainly more reliable than common sense, I found a road that wasn't meant to be there. While the road I wanted to be there was nowhere to be seen.

'You've lost a whole road,' I said to myself, incredulously. 'Not just a turning or a well or a ridge, but a whole bloody road.'

'Take it easy, babe, be calm, she'll be right, mate, settle down settle DOWN.'

My little heart felt like a macaw in a canary cage. I could feel the enormity of the desert in my belly and on the back of my neck. I was not in any real danger – I could easily have set a compass course for Areyonga. But I kept thinking, what if this happens when I'm two hundred miles from anywhere? What if, what if. And I felt very small and very alone suddenly in this great emptiness. I could climb a hill and look to where the horizon shimmered blue into the sky and see nothing. Absolutely nothing.

I reread the map. No enlightenment there. I was only fifteen or so miles from the settlement, and here was this giant dirt highway where there should only be sandstone and roly-poly. Should I follow it or what? I checked the map for mines but there was nothing marked.

I sat back and watched myself perform. 'OK. First of all, you are not lost, you are merely misplaced, no no, you know exactly where you are so stifle that impulse to scream at the camels and kick Diggity. Think clearly. Then, make camp for the night here, there is plenty of green feed, and spend the rest of the afternoon looking for that goddamn track. If you don't find it, cut across country. Easy enough. Above all, do not flap around like a winged pigeon. Where's your pride? Right.'

I did all that, then went off scouting, map in hand, Diggity at foot. I found an ancient trail that wound up through the mountains, not exactly where the map said it should be but close enough for a margin of credibility at least. It went for a couple of miles off course then came out to meet up with, yes, yet another major highway that had no right to exist. This I followed for another half mile in the general direction of Areyonga, until I came across a bullet-ridden piece of tin bent over double and almost rusted away, but with an arrow that pointed at the ground and the letters A ON upon it. I skipped back to camp in the gathering twilight, apologized profusely to my poor dumb entourage, and fixed lesson one firmly in my brain for future reference. When in doubt, follow your nose, trust your instincts, and don't rely on maps.

Travels on My Elephant

Mark Shand

Having decided to travel through India on an elephant, Mark Shand's first problem is finding the right elephant. He begins his search at the zoo...

The long arm of coincidence, in which travellers are often held, found the director of the zoo – the very man for whom I had been given a letter of introduction – travelling on the same flight. There were no elephants that he knew of for sale in Orissa, he told us sympathetically. In fact he himself was looking for elephants both for his own establishment and for a temple. He then suggested we try Madras. 'In the meantime visit my zoo. See the white tigers and the kangaroos that have just arrived from Australia.'

'Well that's that,' I said glumly after we returned to our seats. 'We might as well catch the next flight back to Delhi.' I turned to Aditya, trying to stay calm. 'What on earth are we going to do?' He was fast asleep...

Bhubaneshwar – the city of a thousand temples – was draped in thick black cloud, glistening from the wet kiss of the monsoons. A steamy heat hung in the air. Even the sparrows, those lively occupants of Indian airports, were silent, wilting on top of the announcement speakers.

At the hotel the receptionist asked politely, 'Sands, that is your good name?'

'No, it's Shand.'

'Welcome to the Prachi Hotel, Mr Sands. How long will you be staying?'

'Until I find an elephant'...

As Shand begins to wonder if he will ever make his journey, Aditya returns with the news that he has located some elephants sixty miles away...

'Did they want to sell ?' I asked anxiously.

'We can take our pick. There are two females and one tusker. The tusker comes from Nepal and is a good elephant, or so they tell me. But what the hell do we know about elephants ? We must get some expert advice...'

'What were they like ?'

'Oh, devious b....rs, they...'

'No, no, not the saddhus, the elephants.'

'Big. Like any elephant. I didn't really see them properly. Now let's get some sleep. You'll have plenty of time to look at them tomorrow.'

I found I couldn't sleep. All night everything I looked at became an elephant – the shadow of a swaying branch, the moon-filled clouds or even the television set. My obsession had indeed turned to madness.

It took most of the day to locate the zoo director who kindly agreed to lend the services of his chief mahout, Bhim. Our party had grown. There were now four of us. Myself, Aditya, Mr Tripathy, with his suitcase of elephants, and a young taxi driver called Indrajit, who had impressed Aditya with his driving skills the previous night. He was a handsome, courteous young man, who radiated energy and had dark fierce eyes – the kind of eyes that remain fierce even in jest. But I wasn't thinking about a chauffeur, I was eagerly waiting to set eyes on my first mahout.

In Delhi I had been lent a book on elephants entitled *The Elephant Lore of the Hindus*, which had detailed the essential qualities required in a elephant driver:

The supervisor of elephants should be intelligent, king-like, righteous, devoted to his Lord, pure, true to his undertakings, free from vice, controlling his senses, well behaved, vigorous, tried by practice, delighting in kind words, his science learnt from a good teacher, clever, firm, affording protection, renowned for curing disease, fearless, all-knowing.

The mahout was waiting at the gates of the zoo. Bhim was a man of indeterminate age, the colour of a walnut, bandy-legged and carried himself like a wounded soldier. As we got out of the car he executed a shaky salute, his arm and leg not quite in co-ordination. From the state of his bloodshot eyes, he was clearly suffering from a hangover. He climbed into the car and yawned, exposing the remains of three yellow teeth which wobbled when he spoke. 'Sleep now, sah. Very good. Haathi later.' He then passed out.

Aditya was not wrong about Indrajit. He drove with a cunning recklessness, the tropical landscape passing in a blur outside the window. We had only one accident when he swerved to avoid a bullock cart, clipping the back side-window against one of the animal's enormous horns. The glass exploded like a hand grenade with some of the fragments embedding themselves in Aditya's face. 'Lucky it wasn't my eyes,' he shrugged stoically, picking the glass out of his cheek.

It was late at night by the time we reached Daspalla. The town was deserted. There was no sign of the elephants. I felt as if I had been kicked in the stomach. 'Jesus!' I shouted, 'I just can't believe this. We've lost them. They could be anywhere... '

'No sir,' Mr Tripathy announced calmly, pointing to large mounds like loaves of bread that decorated the road. 'Now we follow shit.'

We pushed on deeper into the night, our eyes glued to the black surface of the road, illuminated in the taxi's headlights, searching for the tell-tale signs. At intervals the trail would run dry and Mr Tripathy and Indrajit would make enquiries. Villagers, rudely awoken by the urgent shouting, would appear in their doorways, cocooned in blankets, looking bewildered and frightened. Reports regarding sightings of the elephants became equally bewildering – anywhere between two hours and six days. We reached a toll gate, where we received more accurate information. The elephants, we were told by the sleepy toll keeper, had definitely passed through. Did he perhaps know how long ago, we asked. No. Unfortunately his watch was not in working order. But he assured us it was not yesterday.

We were closer. The droppings were fresher and, as if on cue, Bhim woke up. 'Haathi close,' he said quietly, rubbing his blood-shot eyes, as he poked his nose out of the window. 'Can smell.'

We rounded the next bend. Three massive shapes loomed out of the night, their shadows dancing over the glow of a small roadside fire, around which lay bundles of vermilion and saffron rags.

'We'll pretend you're a tourist who has never seen an elephant,' Aditya whispered to me. 'Just stare in astonishment.'

As I got out of the car the rags suddenly billowed upwards and I found myself transfixed by three pairs of hot eyes that flashed like cash registers, curtained by matted tresses of long black oily hair. I forgot the necessity of our charade. As if drawn by a magnet, I was already moving towards the elephants.

Then I saw her. My mouth went dry. I felt giddy, breathless. In that moment the ancient wall crumbled and I walked through. With one hind leg crossed over the other, she was leaning nonchantly against a tree, the charms of her perfectly rounded posterior in full view, like a prostitute on a street corner. I knew then that I had to have her. Suddenly, nothing else mattered and I realized with some surprise that I had fallen in love with a female Asian elephant.

As luck would have it, I had become enamoured with a perfect elephant, an elephant, even Bhim said, that made his heart flutter. She was young, between twenty-five and thirty years old and although in poor condition, due to mishandling and starvation, would in fourteen days in his care turn into a lovely riding elephant. She had all the attributes – a healthy pink tongue unblemished by black spots, brown kindly eyes with no traces of white, the right amount of toenails, eighteen, five each on the front feet, four on the back, strong and sturdy joints and a perfect arc to her back. The other two elephants, he warned, were dangerous, and would quite likely kill somebody soon if they hadn't done so already. Take her, he advised me, it would be impossible to find better...

...Even to my inexperienced eye, she appeared to be half starved. She lacked that roundness of girth that I had always associated with elephants. Her rib cage was clearly visible and her skin hung in folds like an ill-fitting suit. She looked at that moment exactly what she was – a beggar. It was only then, as I surveyed this immense bag of bones, that the enormity of the situation struck me. She was mine. I was the owner of an elephant, and the idea seemed so ludicrous that I began to laugh. Quickly I controlled myself for I thought – and this was even more absurd – that she might think I was laughing at her, and I had no desire to hurt her feelings.

I was also at a loss as to how to effect an introduction. She wasn't exactly an average pet, like a cat or a dog, or even a hamster, which one can pick up and cuddle or stroke and expect a contented purr or a wet lick or, in the case of the hamster, a sharp nip. However, she soon solved that problem. As I approached her nervously she stretched out her trunk and with the utmost delicacy began to explore the front of my shirt. She's making friends with me, I thought happily, enchanted by this apparent display of affection. It then stopped abruptly in the area of one of my trouser pockets into which she quickly inserted the tip of her trunk and deftly removed my lunch – an apple – and, with a squeak of delight, popped it into her mouth. It seemed the key to Tara's heart was going to be through her stomach. I dispatched Indrajit to buy her some food.

After two kilos of rice, which she consumed by poking her trunk into the sacks and sucking the contents out like a vacuum cleaner, four bundles of bananas and twenty-three coconuts, she seemed a little more replete and broke wind loudly as if to say thank you. As I watched her crunch up the last of the coconuts, her eyes, fringed by lashes long enough to suggest that they were false, closed contentedly...

From the very moment that Tara took her first step forward, I was filled with a complete sense of security, cocooned, wrapped in cotton-wool. I knew that while this wonderful benign animal lumbered below me, nothing could go wrong. From twelve feet up the view was spectacular. The landscape took on a different perspective and one could see both far and near – the blazing yellow of a distant mustard field or the early morning goings on over a mud wall of a village. But it was the feeling of invincibility that struck me most. My imagination ran riot, and I became the 'King of Bliss' surrounded by a thousand elephants, revelling in the horror and fear of my foes.

The experts told me that it would be uncomfortable, tedious and even painful to travel in a howdah. How wrong they were. I found the soft swaying motion relaxing, almost too relaxing. On occasion, I fell asleep, and just caught myself before I slid off. To prevent this, I fashioned a sling from a length of rope and found I could lie back with my feet hanging over her backside. Then, after plugging in my Walkman, I could recline like a Maharaja, listening to the strains of Italian opera while a huge, never changing empty sky passed by overhead. Occasionally, like a tiny silver arrow, an aeroplane would flash far above. I felt sorry for the passengers squeezed into their pressurized chamber, hurrying from one destination to the next, unable to see the beauty that I was so fortunate to be enjoying. Gradually I was slowing down, slowing down to the pace of a country in which if one moves fast, one misses everything – and like a patient tutor Tara was influencing me, showing me the way.

Between Two Cultures

Smita Patel

Smita Patel, a British Asian woman, took five months off from her job at a feminist publishing house to travel with her boy-friend to India and South East Asia.

This was not my first visit to India. Like most second generation Indians I had been taken to India as a child and young teenager. But these journeys had always been considered as a duty or 'family visit', not as a means of exploring the country or even mixing with the community at large. I had always been aware that as an Indian girl my role was to accept the guidance and protection of my relatives.Returning as an adult independent woman, I knew that I would face problems and dilemmas, and evenmore so travelling with a white boy-friend.

Our trip had been planned as part of wider travels to the East spanning over five months. I was fairly confident about travelling independently (having done so alone and with friends to Europe and Africa) but the warnings of other Asian women surprised and distrubed me. India, I was told, would

be different and travelling with a white partner I should expect much more harassment and abuse. My mind was becoming full of doubts and prejudgements but I drew comfort from the fact that India was a country which has witnessed hordes of travellers of almost every race and nationality, exploring every inch of its land.

I remember arriving at Delhi airport at 3 a.m., feeling apprehensive and excited. I was really no more knowledgeable about what to expect than any other Western traveller. After waiting hours for our baggage we ventured out into 'independent' travelling. It was now 6 a.m. and though the sun had barely risen we were shocked by the sheer volume of people – the first thing you notice about India is how densely populated it is. The whole area outside the airport was packed with families, beggars, police, rickshaw wallahs, fruit vendors, taxi men, and of course the famed hotel sellers, relentlessly directing us to the 'best room in town', as well as countless others trying to attract our attention to sell, buy or give advice. Luckily we had met an American woman on the plane who was being met by her brother who had been living in India for three years, and despite being heavily jet-lagged we managed to struggle out of the chaos and find them. As Ben had been living on a low budget for a year we were soon jostled towards India's cheapest mode of transport, the local bus. It looked ancient and decrepit and I was convinced it would never manage the long ride into Delhi city.

'Even though I had witnessed such scenes as a child and heard of India's poverty, I was still bewildered at the extreme deprivation we came across during our stay.'

In India there are no such things as queues and you learn quickly how to push and shove to get to the front. We piled on to the bus with what seemed like hundreds of others, all Indian, and I gratefully noticed that as a female traveller and a new arrival people would give up their seats to me. Our first impressions were of the sharp images of life glimpsed through the bus window. It took about an hour to reach the city along a road marked by small dwellings and shanty towns made out of paper, cardboard, rubber, tin, in fact anything that the poor could get their hands on. Even though I had witnessed such scenes as a child

and heard of India's poverty, I was still bewildered at the extreme deprivation we were to come across during our stay.

Our first week in Delhi was just as I had visualized it and childhood memories suddenly flooded back. We were staying in the Main Bazaar area of Delhi, near the railway station. This is an old marketplace, full of tiny shops selling everything you could ever need. It's an amazing spectacle of colour and smell, with the persistent noise of fruit and vegetable sellers bargaining over the prices for the day, and rickshaws and bikes swerving through the streets, avoiding the sacred cows that amble in their path. At that stage we were using other travellers' tips and living on a very tight budget. Like most backpackers we tended to be attracted to hotels and eating places where white travellers would meet or end up. To begin with I was unaware that my presence among mostly white men would be seen as strange and immoral behaviour by the Indian men who ran the hotels and eating places.

From the moment of our arrival both Max and I had taken care to dress and act according to Indian customs. At no time did we publicly show affection towards each other such as holding hands, kissing or even being physically close. In England I had been brought up to dress 'respectfully' in the presence of family and community so this was not new to me. However, despite our attempts to merge in I soon discovered that being an Asian woman travelling among independent travellers I was perceived very differently by Indian men. People didn't always notice that I was with a white man, especially if Max and I were looking at different things, but as soon as we were together the stares intensified and men would start making comments and even touching me as they walked past. Understanding Hindi made me aware of all the derogatory comments being made about me.

Sometimes this would lead to more direct harassment, with men changing seats so they could touch me in full view of Max. On one occasion, six men got into the compartment and all took turns to insult me, including trying to sit on my lap. I also often heard men describing white women as loose and sexually available. It was clear that to them I was a 'white product', a British-born woman doing what mostly white women do, flaunting my independence by travelling around with a white man.

'It was clear that to them I was a 'white product', a British-born woman doing what mostly white women do, flaunting my independence.'

We also experienced men approaching Max and talking about me as though I was invisible and had no mind of my own. I was made to feel like an appendage, passive and speaking only through him. Towards the end of our travels I had given up trying to explain my own point of view and simply let Max do all the talking. I felt caught between differing values, having to play an uneasy shifting game of what was expected from an Indian woman. As a child growing up in an Indian family I had experienced a similar 'balancing out' of values and had learnt intuitively when to be silent. In India I was silent again, superficially accepting men's behaviour towards me simply to get through a hassle-free day of travelling. But this passivity became much harder as time wore on. Things came to a head in Varanasi, where after only three days I had been subjected to so much abuse and harassment that I retreated to my hotel room and wept. I knew this was not an overreaction or paranoia as white travellers had noticed and commented on how differently I was being treated.

I was left with the feeling that perhaps the two different sides of me just did not fit into Indian life. My attempts to cover up my feminism and, by taking a passive role, to try and gain the approval of Indian men, soon gave way to overwhelming feelings of resentment. It was mortifying when I realized that I was dismissing part of my own culture in a way that can only be described as racist. Unfortunately, being so isolated from other Indian women – I experienced little or no contact with them – my experiences in India were very much male dominated.

These extremely harassing times were also contrasted with some blissfully relaxed moments. After leaving India to spend a while trekking in the Himalayas we returned to spend our last three weeks in Kashmir and Ladakh. Kashmir is known as a tourist attraction and in the month of June many Indians themselves leave the hot plains to cool off in the Kashmir hills. We headed for Dal lake and found a house run by an old Kashmiri man who was obviously respected in the community. We were taken under his family's wing and I experienced no sexual harassment during the stay; due mainly, I am sure, to the fact that his many relatives acknowledged and therefore protected us.

Travelling around India I learnt what it felt like to be an outsider in a culture which I regard as my roots. My experiences, however, were very much my own and I really couldn't say how much they'd apply to other British Asian women travellers. Certainly, the prejudice we encountered as a mixed race couple is not confined to India alone. Returning to England left me in complete culture shock and finding my bearings in British society has again taken time.

Among the Russians

Colin Thubron

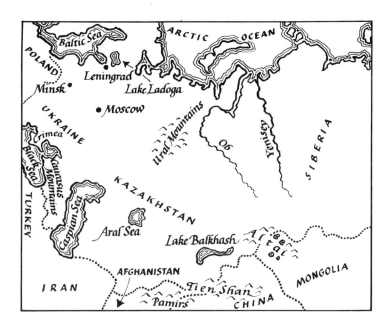

I had been afraid of Russia ever since I could remember. When I was a boy its mass dominated the map which covered the classroom wall; it was tinted a wan green, I recall, and was distorted by Mercator's projection so that its tundras suffocated half the world. Where other nations – Japan, Brazil, India – clamoured with imagined scents and colours, Russia gave out only silence, and was somehow incomplete. I grew up in its shadow, just as my parents had grown up in the shadow of Germany.

Journeys rarely begin where we think they do. Mine, perhaps, started in that classroom, where the green-tinted mystery hypnotized me during maths lessons. Already questions rose in the child's mind: why did this country seem stranger, less explicit, than others? Why was it untranslated into any precise human expression? The questions were half-formed, of course, but the fear was already there.

Perhaps it was because of this that thirty years later the land glimmering eastward from the Polish frontier struck me as both familiar and foreboding. It flowed away in an undifferentiated calm, or rose and fell so imperceptibly that only the faintest lift of the horizon betrayed it. I saw nobody. The sky loomed preternaturally vast. The whole world seemed to have been crushed and flattened out into a numinous peace. My car sounded frail on the road. For three hours it had been disembowelled by border officials at Brest, and its faultily-replaced door panels rasped and squealed as if they enclosed mice.

Even now I was unsure what drew me into this country I feared. I belonged to a generation too young to romanticize about Soviet Communism. Yet nothing in the intervening years had dispelled my childhood estrangement and ignorance. My mind was filled with confused pictures: paradox, cliché. 'Russia,' wrote the Marquis de Custine in 1839, 'is a country where everyone is part of a conspiracy to mystify the foreigner.' Propaganda still hangs like a ground-mist over the already complicated truth. Newspapers, until you know how to read them, are organs of disinformation. The arts are conservative or silent. Even in novels, which so often paint the ordinary nature of things, the visionaries and drunks who inhabit the pages of nineteenth century fiction have shrivelled to the poor wooden heroes of modern socialist realism. It is as if a great lamp had been turned down.

As for me, I was entering the country too impatiently to be well equipped. I spoke a hesitant Russian, but had read very little. And I was deeply prejudiced. Nobody from the West enters the Soviet Union without prejudice. I took in with me, as naturally as the clothes I wore, a legacy of individualism profoundly different from anything east of the Vistula.

But I think I wanted to know and embrace this enemy I had inherited. I felt myself, at least a little, to be on his side. Communism at once attracted and repelled me. Nothing could be more alluring to the puritan idealist whose tatters (I suppose) hung about me as I took the road to Minsk; nothing more disquieting to the solitary. All my motives, when I thought about them, filled up with ambiguity. Even my method of travel was odd. The Russians favour transient groups and delegations, which are supervised in grandiose hotels. But I was going alone, in my own car, staying at campsites, and planned to cover ten thousand miles along almost every road permitted to me (and a few which were not) between the Baltic and the Caucasus. My head was swimming in contradictory expectations. A deformed grandeur still hovered about this nation in my eyes.

So for more than two hundred miles between Brest and Minsk, I travelled in a state of nervous fascination. There was almost nothing else on the road: dust-clogged lorries carrying wood, cement, cattle; a rare bus; and once a truck packed with frosty-eyed Brueghel peasantry. Every twenty miles or so, in glass and concrete checkpoints raised above the highway, grey-uniformed police fingered their binoculars and telephones. The land was haunted by absences – no advertisements, no pylons, often no telegraph poles. The cluttered country of industrial Europe was smoothed out into a magisterial stillness. Grass-lands, farmlands, forests. All huge, all silent. The eye could never compass any one of them. The forests, in particular, looked deep and unredeemed. They lapped against fields and roads in rich, deciduous masses of oak, beech, silver birch. This was Belorussia, 'White Russia', a state of rye and timberland which stretched half-way to Moscow. The deadening pine forests still lingered about its pastures and stencilled every horizon in a line of coniferous darkness.

I gazed at all this with the passion of a newcomer, and scribbled it in a diary before I should forget the feel of ordinary, important things. These first hours shone with a peculiar intensity. In the fields of potato and alfalfa, labourers moved through a soft July sunlight – men and stout women in headscarves wielding billhooks and pitchforks. No collectivized glamour, no tractors or combine harvesters intruded into the sodden ritual of their haymaking. Instead, where marshy fields elbowed through the forests, black and white cattle grazed in isolated herds, and troops of herons paced nonchalantly across the meadows.

After a hundred miles I stopped the car and lay on the verge among butterflies and lupins. The country was steeped in silence. In this limitless terrain, details of plant or insect shone with the exposed distinctness of things seen in the desert. A dragonfly clattered onto my knee. Bright yellow toadflax squeezed up between my fingers. They were obscurely comforting.

But I was conscious above all of the stunned desolation which seems to permeate these plains. It has to do, I think, less with their actual poverty – sandy soil, poor drainage – than with the inarticulate vastness of which they form a part. Without the nearness of towns or the presence of hills, the sky takes on a terrible passive force. Stand anywhere here, and three-quarters of your field of vision is engulfed by it, adding a pitiless immensity to the size of the land. The sun and clouds hang permanent and immobile in its blue. They curve above you like a Tiepolo ceiling. Everything beneath is exposed. The weather itself assumes a threatening, total quality, so that the earth can momentarily wither under a flagellating sun, and rain burst like a cataclysm. Above all, people – their houses, traffic, cattle – grow pitifully incidental. The villages I passed generally stood far off the road – wooden cottages with asbestos or tin roofs pitched steep against snow. They were small, abstract – a civilization sketched puny in the fields, like a language I didn't know. Its people, it seemed, were not enclosed and nurtured, made private or different by the folds of valleys and mountains. They were figures in a landscape, living under the naked sky in the glare of infinity.

Driving eastward through this anonymity, I became obsessed by the sheer magnitude of the country I was trying to pierce. Larger than South America, two and a half times bigger than the

United States, it extends half-way round the globe and contains one sixth of the land surface of the whole earth. My own journey – eastward to Moscow, north to Leningrad and the Baltic Sea, south to the Caucasus and the Turkish border, back across the Ukraine and the Crimea – comprised only the historic edge of a mighty wilderness. If I traced an imaginary line eastward from where I was driving, it would move for more than a thousand miles over country nearly identical to this, where the altitude changes by no more than 980 feet until the Ural Mountains. Another thousand-mile line extending south-east would meet the black earth and grasslands of the steppes, which I would reach that autumn. But the Soviet Union here has barely begun. Eastward again the black earth pales into the deserts of Kazakhstan, where in summer the temperature may stand at 105°F in the shade for weeks at a time. For hundreds of miles the earth is tossed into dunes or sets hard as a parquet floor, and the rivers wind into landlocked seas or die of exhaustion across the sands. Northward, in the valleys of the Ob river, spreads the hugest lowland on earth – the mosquito-plagued lakes and swamplands of the West Siberian plain, while eastward again lies the forbidding heart of this whole continent: Central Siberia, bounded by the glacial waters of the Arctic Ocean.

It is these Siberian lands – ice-glazed, wind-stricken – which sit behind the inner eye as you drive east. They lend their invisible enormity to everything around you. While I was driving here at midday, their farther reaches were still plunged in night. In the far north – land of the reindeer and snowy owl – three months of winter go by without daylight at all, and the mean winter temperature is −60°F, the coldest of all habitable regions of the world. The rivers and the very seas freeze in corridors and oceans of ice. Even in summer the tundra subsoil is perpetually frozen, and the sun squeezes from the earth only a liquid mud, where bulbs flower in a fleeting gasp of scent. Across the wastes of southern Siberia, in a region huger than Canada, more than two and a half million square miles of stunted conifers, larches and birches surround rivers which are barely known – the Yenisei, gouging out a passage 3,600 miles into the Arctic; the

Lena, which already measures twenty miles across in its middle course and floods 2,550 miles into a delta which is ice-choked even in August. The very girdle of mountains massed along these southern fringes echoes with unreachable names – the Pamirs and the Tien Shan whose peaks are among the highest in the world, the Altai scattered with translucent lakes, and mountain chains still farther east which only peter out in the tiger-prowled heights along the Chinese border, and in Kamchatka's Pacific peninsula.

All this lent a majestic and dwarfing dimension to my journey. Already the country was cast in the mould of those imagined tundras and rivers. It was slow, impersonal and absolute. I could not help wondering what effect such isolation might have on its inhabitants – the lack of visual stimuli, of anything varied or unique in the landscape at all. Was the easy Russian submissiveness to God or tyranny, I wondered, the result of a people crushed by the sheer size of their land? Could it be that the meandering, mystical, rough-hewn qualities of the Russian psyche – Russian novels, Russian music – that the unwieldly immensity of Russian bureaucracy...

But this froth of irresponsible questions subsided unanswered at a sign which said 'Minsk Campsite'.

Sequins for a Ragged Hem

Amryl Johnson

Returning to her roots in the Caribbean, Amryl Johnson encounters some unexpected forms of entertainment...

I was about to witness goat racing. A little later, there would be crab racing. Easter Monday in Buccoo Village. I was fighting my way through ice-cream vans, hoards of people, food stalls and hot music singeing my eardrums. Even though the general movement was towards the racecourse, I elbowed my way through the crowds in an effort to get a good pitch. An area had been cordoned off to make a course for competitors. Not quite on a par with the traditional racing scale but on a parallel assumption that spectators were to line either side of a stretch of ground along which the participants would travel.

I was not too sure who I was with. Neither Rita nor Kelvin were with me.

'Girl, I stopped going two years ago. If you see it once you see it a million time.'

Joinie took me to Buccoo Village before going back to work. Gingo and Stylas performed a sort of tag match. They were in an all-male group nearby, drinking and playing cards. I had been walking around the site, soaking in the atmosphere and enjoying being on my own. They would find me from time to time to phrase a variation of the same question.

'You want anything? You want ice-cream, sweet bread, roti, a plate of stewed beef and rice, souse, black pudding, sugar cake, beer, mauby ?'

A faraway look of concentration on their faces as hands delved into pockets to fish out coins or peel off a note which they felt corresponded to my culinary requirements. I told them yes to the first question and no to the rest. Rita was an excellent cook. I had had more than my fair share of breakfast that morning. Salt fish cooked with tomatoes and onions, washed down with a big cup of real chocolate was a heavier breakfast than I was used to. However, I was quickly getting accustomed to the change.

Some people take this event very seriously. I have been told that money changes hands. 'The goats are looking frisky'. I wish I could have used that expression to describe what I saw. The glazed preoccupation of the goats as they stood chewing their cuds made them look anything but 'frisky'. You will not find jockeys seated on their mounts here. Good job too! Feel sure they would have the Tobagonian equivalent of the RSPCA down on them like a ton of bricks. An attempt was being made to keep a handful of select goats in order. No mean achievement when dealing with an animal fabled to eat almost anything it can lay its mouth to. Around each animal's neck was a rope. At the end of each rope was a man holding a stick. Part of the uniform looked authentic. The trousers were white, near white, off white, and looked the sort of clothes you would expect to be worn by anyone taking part in an exercise of that nature. In that respect one could call the men minders. Bare feet, teeshirt or vest, identification number completed the ensemble.

And they were off! I soon got the idea. It was how quickly you and your quadruped could race the other men and theirs to the finishing line. Bare feet and hooves pounded stones further into the ground. The humans were moving as if their lives depended on it. The goats were probably certain their lives did. Curried goat is a delicacy on the islands. First one across the line got cooked? Or was it the last one to cross who went into the pot? Either way, it would be best to play safe and stay close to the middle. The tension on the rope was nail-biting. There is always one. There is always one soul who remains oblivious to ruin. The hooves of one billy were thudding on the quaking earth as if his life would begin when he reached the finishing line. His minder looked a worried man. He had reason. His feet had hardly touched the ground since the race began. He was hanging on to the end of the rope with both hands – must be some sort of life raft – and being tugged to the finishing line. He was declared the winner. Rumour had it the goat ended up in the pot, anyway. They had to throttle it to get it to stop running. The minder responded to everyone who congratulated him with the same surprised, bewildered smile.

Crab racing turned out to be even more of an inspiration. I don't know how long it had been since the creatures left their natural habitat but they looked as if they had resigned themselves to their fate. Even if the barrel they had just been taken from contained sea water or, alternatively, mud from their very own swamp, all memory of home had now gone. They languished in the afternoon sun as if they hadn't a care in the world. Since ropes would be ridiculous on creatures that size, a sturdy piece of string was attached to the anatomy of each crustacean. The minders spent much time in examining claws and paying attention to details. In addition to the string, there was a second prop. It was one which could be described as the urging and steering mechanism – a stick.

When the race began I tried not to rationalize or demand too much logic from what was taking place. But it was madness to the nth degree. A number of male adults were holding a piece of string. At the other end of the string was a crab. The men were endeavouring to urge the creatures forward at a satisfactory pace with the aid of the stick. One crab was going backwards and continued to do so regardless of any attempts to the contrary.

Three of them appeared to be moving diagonally. Two others seemed to be dancing a quadrille.

As always, there was a maverick. Slowly but surely he was inching forward. The crab was moving slowly but surely towards the finishing line. It was not so much a race as an exercise in patience. Not far removed from taking your pet snail for a walk. There was no longer any reason to scuttle. When you scuttle, you move with some intent to escape. If you are tethered by a string and the radius of your movement is governed by its length, then what's the point? These crustaceans, in any case, looked as if they no longer knew the meaning of the word scuttle. Even worse, some seemed to be experiencing difficulty in moving a claw forward. I didn't know the rules of the race. Were there any? Was it my imagination or did I notice some tugging on the string? It would obviously serve to pull the crab forward at a speed not of its own volition. My eyes were riveted on the maverick some short distance from the finishing line.

The spectators were better behaved than the ones in Trinidad. However, one or two began voicing their doubts about the precise physical condition of the winner.

'You damn cheat!'

'The crab dead! All you can't see the crab dead?!!'

I felt the protestors had a point. The only movement from the crab was the involuntary one made by any motion of the string.

'How all you people so blasted stupid? All you can't see the crab already dead when he haul it across the line?!'

This was very interesting. The crab went into a series of jerks as the minder worked the string to demonstrate it was still in the land of the living. Alternatively, it could indeed have been involuntary. Death throes.

'How man in he right mind go want pin medal on dead crab?!'

Howls of laughter from the spectators. The winner sat unconcerned. Surely rigor mortis had now set in. At any rate, no attempt was being made to lift a claw in triumphant acclamation of victory.

'And I say it dead before it cross the line!'

A number of people formed a circle around the winner. There was much close inspection going on.

'He move! I see he move!'

It was confirmed by another person in the circle. There was

much jubilation. Everyone seemed happy. Everyone, that is, except the crab. And while we settled down to enjoy the rest of the afternoon, I was left with my doubts. Was there life in that body when the first claw slithered across the line?

My next encounter with them was the following day.

'Well, you just miss something.'

I walked into the house to be greeted by Joinie full of smiles. After the shock of that first evening, I was always very interested in what he wore. Mercifully, nothing came close to rivalling those shorts.

'If you did come half hour sooner you would have really see something.'

Rita came out of the kitchen, hands on hips.

'Girl, if you know what now, now happen to me.'

Moses came out of the kitchen sucking on a mango. He took his lips from the pulp long enough to set the scene.

'We walk in here to find a crab chasing she round the kitchen.'

Rita held one hand at a distance from the other in what might, at first, suggest an angler's tale. She narrowed the distance.

'And if you see the size of the thing.'

She grabbed my arm.

'Come, let me show you.'

I put my head round the kitchen to find Moses now almost down to the seed and still assaulting the mango with relish. On the draining board lay a mangled crab. The claws and back were indeed enormous.

'Moses had to kill the bitch.'

She became thoughtful for a few seconds.

'I feel is the same one that did do for Kelvin.'

They caught the crabs in the swamps. The men would shine torches on them late at night. The light would make the crabs active. As they scuttled to get out of the artificial sunshine, the men would grab and put them in the sack. Kelvin lost his grip on one. Trying to retrieve it, the claws sank into his shoulder cutting through the teeshirt. All this had happened the night before. I did not see the gash. I heard the next morning. Moses and Joinie were laughing and joking about the sight of the mother and father of all crabs chasing Rita round the kitchen. I never got to the bottom of it but it seemed as if the sack they were in was not properly tied or else there was a hole in it.

'Girl, I suddenly hear this noise. When I look down I see this thing coming. I never see a thing that size in my life. I start to run. How you mean? You think I so stupid I going to stand still?'

'He was coming for you, was he?'

'How you mean? The thing coming, coming.'

I tried to keep a straight face.

'Well, he probably wanted revenge. He must have heard of all the things you've been doing to his grandchildren in the name of sport.'

When Pele Blows, the Lava Flows

Greg Ward

It seems that only Europeans still have illusions about Hawaii. For Americans, it is where you go for your honeymoon or if you win the lottery, with all the luxury hotels, air-conditioning and fast-food of home. Only two centuries ago these islands were unknown specks in the Pacific, 2,000 miles from the nearest land; today their population of 1.1 million is much the same as when Captain Cook arrived, but fewer than 10,000 of the inhabitants are pure-blood Hawaiians.

The story of how Hawaii was taken from the Polynesians and amalgamated into the United States is quite outrageous – even the US President at the time called it 'wholly without justification' – but, none the less, it is a *fait accompli*. Mainlanders with an eye for business are still streaming in (only to wax indignant now the Japanese are doing the same), and much of what was unique and indigenous – culturally, ecologically, you name it – has gone.

But if you do go to Hawaii expecting something extraordinary, and are prepared to look beyond Honolulu and Waikiki Beach, it can be found. On any of the islands you come upon landscapes of quite stunning beauty, but what really blew me away – almost literally – was the primeval power of the volcanoes of Hawaii itself. Much the biggest of the islands, and known simply as the Big Island, Hawaii is one of the least touristy. Its sheer size makes it possible to keep well away from the few resorts.

Each of the Hawaiian islands has been thrust 20,000 feet up from the ocean floor by the successive eruptions of submarine volcanoes. As each island in turn drifts away from the 'hot spot' on the sea bed, its volcano dies and it sinks back into the sea. The Big Island is the newest of them all, with two volcanoes of over 13,000 feet, and it is still growing. As the director of Hawaii Volcanoes National Park assured me, 'It's alive. It changes. Every day there's something new.'

We were at the crater of Kilauea volcano, about 7,000 feet and 20 miles up from the ocean, but another 7,000 feet below the summit of giant Mauna Loa, where several major observatories take advantage of the world's clearest atmosphere. 'Sure, the air's clean up there; down here you can chew on it.' Downwind of the crater, they get 150 inches of acid rain each year and no plants grow. A couple of miles away, upwind, there is a tropical rainforest.

Mark Twain described this crater as a dazzling lake of fire; I was hiding my disappointment at finding it a desert. 'But you're so lucky,' said the park director, 'you're here at exactly the right time to see something Mark Twain would have given his eye-teeth to see – the volcano is erupting right into the ocean, you can hike out there and watch it happen.' I asked how long this had been going on. 'Eight years.' If, after eight years, he was still falling off his seat with glee at the thought of it, the least I could do was change my plans and miss an appointment with the manager of a distant nut plantation.

The Chain of Craters road winds from the park HQ down to the sea. If Hawaii is the place where they paved paradise and put up a parking lot, then here paradise is fighting back. Fresh sheets of lava are constantly oozing down the slopes and covering the road. When they build the road again, more lava covers it. From high on the hillside it looks like a stream of black Tarmac, an ever-widening highway down to the endless blue ocean.

The volcano's power to destroy and create at random is awesome. New land is added day by day. A new beach of jet-black sand was created overnight in January 1988, after an eruption out at sea. There it was the next morning; two miles long, utterly pristine.

Whole towns have been engulfed; no one is sure where they are buried, as there is nowhere for the surveyors to get their bearings. There are no towns left on the southern coast. The Hawaiians abandoned their villages 150 years ago after a succession of terrible tidal waves; now the Americans, too, have been driven out.

I parked my car where the Chain of Craters road runs into a solid wall of lava. A ranger in a wooden shack on wheels – I could see its tracks vanishing under the blackness – handed me a reassuring leaflet saying new lava is unstable and may collapse at any time, and it is best to avoid clouds of hydrochloric acid.

I set off towards the distant columns of steam that marked the hot spot. There is no path, you just pick your way through broken slabs and steam hissing from gashes in the rock. Every surface is like sandpaper, a simple fall can shred your skin.

For ancient Hawaiians, the volcano goddess Pele was the most capricious of deities; priests tested their spiritual strength (*mana*) by controlling her outbursts. Sacred sites also could possess *mana*. One of the oldest temples in Hawaii stands undamaged in the midst of this wasteland, the only man-made structure to survive.

A few miles away, the Christian church was moved bodily out of the way before its *mana* could be put to the test. The Temple of the Red-mouthed God stayed put, relying on an impeccable five-century record of human sacrifice to Pele. It was built on the highest ground around, and perhaps it is not surprising that the lava flowed to either side and left it untouched. Presumably someone also has a good explanation for the cold wind that swirls round the sacrificial platform when all else is still.

I found myself standing about 10 feet above the waves on a ledge of black lava. Down at sea level, a sluggish river of orange and yellow rock churned into the water, sending up plumes of steam and evil smelling gases, and exploding as it hit the water. This river had been flowing some unspecified distance below the thin crust across which I had just walked.

I stayed there until the sun went down and the molten glow of the lava was the only light. A succession of hikers came towards the conflagration, prodding with sticks at the eggshell crust. It is hard to know what made us all ignore the notice-boards: 'Extreme danger: Do not go beyond this point'. People – especially the eternally self-confident Americans – seem to consider themselves impregnable. Somehow nature concurs; there has yet to be a serious injury after eight years of such nocturnal rambles.

A small cone of fine ash had formed at the seafront, half of which had dropped into the molten river below. It was not the most stable of structures to climb; my feet sank in deep on every step and sent a fine powder slithering around me. From the top I looked down 20 feet into a fiery orange pool, gently bubbling and popping, sending up little spouts and phlegmy strings of rock.

There were three or four other people nearby, silhouetted against the orange clouds. A sudden thud made my knees buckle. As I turned, the volcano below nonchalantly vomited a shower of rocks into the air above me. Now I felt entitled to break into a run, although wading through volcanic ash in the dark felt more like a slow-motion nightmare. As I ran I was half-aware that it was pure luck whether one hit me.

As it turned out, a glowing boulder larger than my head thumped down six feet away from me. I crept back to examine it, bright orange on the black moon-scape. Then, after a brief attempt to elicit sympathy for my brush with death from a couple of faceless strangers, I stumbled away through the night.

Tourists

How to Speak Brochurese

Keith Waterhouse

The key to all holiday brochures is the picture of the hotel swimming-pool. What you see is it. There isn't any more. Although the water laps the edge of the photograph to give you the impression that there's twice as much pool if only they had the space to show it, a millimetre more and you would see dry land. That peculiar triangle shape is not a segment of a huge Olympic-sized pool. It is a complete, close-cropped representation of a peculiarly triangular-shaped pool.

The same goes for bedrooms, where the photograph likewise contrives to suggest that there is a lot more room to the east of the twin beds. There isn't. When the photographer took that picture, it was with his back pressed up against the wall, or inside the wardrobe if that is not shown.

The bird's eye view of the beach looks inviting. The reason it's a bird's eye view is that shooting from a few feet back on the hotel roof, the camera avoids the four-lane highway that your balcony overlooks.

But anyone booking a holiday solely on the recommendation of a brochure, particularly a tour operator's brochure, must be suffering from anticipatory heatstroke. The only real use of a brochure, apart from giving you a vague idea what a resort looks like with the abattoir obliterated (that's why the picture is L-shaped) is to convey the only solid information it contains, which is the price. This is the one area in which the brochure cannot lie – or anyway, not much. A hundred metres in brochurese may mean half a mile, and two mins may mean ten mins, but £246 for fourteen days means £246 for fourteen days – plus, of course, the fuel surcharge you may be asked for even though the strength of the pound against the dollar has brought fuel prices down.

To find out what the place is really like, consult a guide book, which as well as mentioning the prominence of the abattoir will probably also list the hotels, with a no-frills summary of their amenities and a clear indication of their position on, or off, the town map. If this information is too skimpy, consult a hotel guide for the region if there is one, and if there isn't, talk to your travel agent. Some holiday specialists, notably Hogg Robinson and Lunn Poly, put out their own hotel guides which, while not quite in the same class for frankness as the old Roy Brooks house ads ('Second bedroom, suit dwarf but no cat-swingers please') are engagingly impartial. Other agents have their own under-the-counter guide books and in response to direct questions, such as 'Look, does "within easy reach of airport" mean it's built on the edge of the runway or not?', they may give you a direct answer. If they give you an evasive one ('The only other information we have is that it has unobstructed views of the distant mountains'), there is something to hide.

You may, at the end of the day, be driven back to the brochure: in which case it is as well to have a smattering of brochurese. A Concise Dictionary of Brochurese follows:

ALL WITH BATH OR SHOWER – yours is with shower.

AMENITIES – noun used to make what is singular sound plural, e.g. shopping amenities = shop.

BRAND-NEW COMPLEX – unfinished.

BUFFET-STYLE – queues.

BUSTLING HOTEL IN ONE OF THE LIVELIEST AREAS – conga line under your window at 3 a.m.

CLOSE TO NIGHTLIFE (OR NITELIFE) – over disco.

COLOURFUL – fruit and veg.

COMMANDING VIEWS – up a steep hill.

COMPLIMENTARY COCKTAIL ON ARRIVAL – ill-printed voucher on arrival, which may be exchanged in bar for foul green drink.

COURTESY COACH TO POINTS OF INTEREST – out in the sticks, no buses.

EXTENSIVELY RENOVATED – concrete mixer on sun-deck.

FACILITIES – do-it-yourself, as in tea-making facilities (no room service), drying facilities (no laundry), conference facilities (underground room with slide projector).

FEW (as in few minutes from) – many.

FRIENDLY ATMOSPHERE – slack service.

GENTLE SLOPE – one-in-three gradient.

INFORMAL – bare chests at breakfast.

INTERNATIONAL CUISINE – melon boats.

JOLLY ATMOSPHERE – raucous.

JUST MINUTES AWAY – bus every half hour.

KING-SIZED (as in double bed) – no room for queen.

LIVELY – full of *Sun* readers.

MANY (as in many other attractions) – few.

MODERN – concrete egg-box.

MODERNIZED – bedroom sliced up to accommodate shower unit.

NO FRILLS – bring your own coathangers.

NOT THE RITZ – not even the Station Hotel.

OVERLOOKING – used strictly in the sense of ignoring, hence overlooking sea means overlooking railway lines in between.

QUIET LOCATION – in outer suburbs.

RELAXING MAÑANA STYLE – utter incompetence.

REFURBISHED – lowered ceiling, concealed lighting.

SECLUDED – round a corner.

SIMPLY FURNISHED – plywood fittings.

SPECTACULAR SCENERY – half-way up a mountain.

STRIKING – ugly.

SUN-DRENCHED – hot.

THRIVING – overcrowded.

TWO MAGNIFICENT POOLS – two small pools, one of them drained.

VALUE FOR MONEY – read small print.

VIRTUALLY ON EXCELLENT SANDY BEACH – across road from building blocking view of excellent sandy beach.
WILL BE PART OF THE AMENITIES – not yet built.
WITHIN WALKING DISTANCE – cab-ride.

1 brochure metre	= 3 metres
1 brochure minute	= 5 minutes
1 brochure person (as in 'sleeps six')	= 1 half-person

Holiday Advertisements: Jersey

94

Postcard from Epcot

Clive James

A technological fun-fair made possible by the microprocessor
and mankind's allegedly unflagging responsiveness to the cuddly
warmth of Mickey Mouse, Epcot is the Walt Disney organization's latest and most awe-inspiring addition to the large part of
central Florida known as the Vacation Kingdom. From the
moment I first heard about Epcot I knew I would do almost
anything to get out of going there, but duty called...

...As one who must watch his weight lest it double overnight, I
was chastened to be in the presence of a whole population whose
idea of weight-watching is to watch other people's weight while
adding to their own. Imperfectly circular men and women clad in
T-shirts and running shorts snacked their way through one-
pound bags of peanut brittle. They all wore training shoes.
Training for what? A heart attack? That the rides should keep
breaking down no longer seemed quite such a mystery.

Inside the pavilion there was a hundred-piece multi-screen
movie plus stereo song. 'Ener-gee! Bringing our world new
graces!' Then we went through into an environment of rhubarb
lurex drapes with blocks of seats looking like cut-down buses
minus wheels. 'You are seated in an Epcot innovation, the
Travelling Theater,' said a tape proudly. 'Keep your hands and
arms inside the vehicle at all times.' Another wrap-around movie
told us about energy in the past. Then the screen rolled up and
we rumbled forward to see what the past looked like.

'Come with us', boomed a doomy tape, 'into the Mesozoic
age.' 'Where we *goin*'?' asked the large lady filling the row of
seats beside me. 'Oh my! Whoo-*ee*! Lookit *that*!' The Mesozoic
turned out to be a block-long diorama with dinosaurs looming
out of dry-ice fumes. Chips and solenoids gave the embattled
beasts a more subtle repertoire of movement than the standard

Disneyland animated dummies with which we have long been familiar. Instead of moving their heads from side to side and their arms up and down, they moved their heads up and down as well as from side to side, while moving their arms from side to side as well as up and down. More interesting was that the all-powerful Epcot master computer had failed to close the automatic doors in my section of the Travelling Theater, so there was a chance that if my companion breathed out suddenly I might be propelled into the Mesozoic, there to be engulfed by primeval steam.

On through the hologram-haunted and diode-decorated darkness grumbled the solar-powered, computer-guided Travelling Theater, with the sound system thundering a continuous testament to 'the genius of the human mind'. But as the Travelling Theater headed out of the prehistoric jungle and back into the era of the rhubarb lurex drapes, suddenly the whole show ground to a halt. '*Mmwah mmwah!*' said the Travelling Theater, going nowhere. 'Please remain seated,' said a human voice. 'We are experiencing operating difficulties.'

The tape moved on to its next cue, which was now out of sequence with events. 'Welcome back, folks! We hope... *click*.' The computer must have forgotten to tell the cassette-player to hit the pause key. An Imagineer appeared out of the mist, lifted up a panel in the Travelling Theater, and doctored the hardware. '*Mmwah!*' Still no action. 'We are unable', said the human voice, 'to continue with our presentation.' The brochure told us what we had missed. 'The forces of energy and the part they play in our lives is powerfully depicted in the show's final act.' It sounded good...

Next, Clive James moves to the World Showcase, where areas devoted to different countries lie side by side, allowing visitors to sample contrasting cultures. James is not impressed...

...What the Walt Disney World needs is a sense of humour, which can't be had without facing facts. Despite Epcot's much-vaunted educational value, it teaches very little worth learning, because it empties the significance from any subject before beginning to expound it. The World Showcase is not a model of tomorrow's harmonious international society. It is a model of nothing except itself. Real countries aren't like that. They have conflicts of interest within themselves and between each other, and always will have. The most they can hope for is to resolve their differences. The message that they should choose peace is not a message. It is empty talk.

So is the message that we can choose our future. The choice is not up to us – not because there is no choice but because there is no us. In its confident assumption that there can be such a thing as a collective will, the Walt Disney World provides democracy's version of totalitarianism – miniaturized instead of monolithic, kindly instead of cruel, but equally drained of all nuance. For real laughter to happen, reality must break through. Most of the laughter I have ever heard in the various branches of the Walt Disney World has been hollow, even from the children. A vast organization which tells you how to have fun is not the same as an individual being funny.

Walt Disney was funny. If you didn't think him that, at least you couldn't deny that he was creative. Critics who said that his creations were in bad taste missed the point. Genius is often in bad taste. They should have said that he was, at his frequent worst, tasteless – in the sense that a Gormay Meal is all presentation but tastes of nothing. ('A generous portion of tender minute-sized shrimp,' said the menu from which I chose my last Gormay Meal in the Vacation Kingdom, 'doing the backstroke on a sea of lettuce, lemon crown, tomato, olives and egg quarters.') But at least Disney's creatures, no matter how excruciatingly adorable, were to some extent the expression of a single human mind...

...You should see Epcot if you are ever in the Vacation Kingdom, but the best reason for ever being in the Vacation Kingdom is Sea World, whose dolphins and whales remind you that man's creative genius is by no means the greatest thing in creation. The Walt Disney World without Walt Disney is a vision without imagination – the very quality it congratulates itself on possessing in abundance. It is the echo of a lost voice, a message from the past that welcomes an empty future. 'The challenge of tomorrow... to reach out and fulfil our *squawk.*' Dreams.

Betjemanesque

Simon Rae

For the End of the Holiday

Silly hats and rolled-up beach mats,
    Duty Free and peeling shins;
Memories of epic evenings,
    Cameras crammed with rueful grins.

Turbulence both in and outside
    Makes for upsets on the flight.
Start the way you mean to finish,
    Ie: start completely tight.

As she rolls the clinking trolley
    Catch the stewardess's eye;
Fear of flying's like a fever:
    One more scotch before we die.

Miles and miles below us, England
    Mottled in the summer sun;
Suddenly the angles alter:
    Our descent has just begun.

Rows of houses like a street map,
    Cars and buses clear as day;
Hope our pilot picks the right one —
    Heathrow, not the motorway.

Captain Confident's smooth talking,
    Calm above the engines' din,
Reassures the nervous fliers.
    Now, he says, we're going in.

Suddenly we lose our bearings
    As we bank through thick grey cloud;
Hearts in mouths we touch the tarmac;
    We swirl in the jostling crowd.

Reunited with our baggage
    At the airport terminus
We are safe, fatigued, impatient,
    Waiting for the Avis bus.

To the Sea

Philip Larkin

To step over the low wall that divides
Road from concrete walk above the shore
Brings sharply back something known long before —
The miniature gaiety of seasides.
Everything crowds under the low horizon:
Steep beach, blue water, towels, red bathing caps,
The small hushed waves' repeated fresh collapse
Up the warm yellow sand, and further off
A white steamer stuck in the afternoon —

Still going on, all of it, still going on!
To lie, eat, sleep in hearing of the surf
(Ears to transistors, that sound tame enough
Under the sky), or gently up and down
Lead the uncertain children, frilled in white
And grasping at enormous air, or wheel
The rigid old along for them to feel
A final summer, plainly still occurs
As half an annual pleasure, half a rite,

As when, happy at being on my own,
I searched the sand for Famous Cricketers,
Or, farther back, my parents, listeners
To the same seaside quack, first became known.
Strange to it now, I watch the cloudless scene:
The same clear water over smoothed pebbles,
The distant bathers' weak protesting trebles
Down at its edge, and then the cheap cigars,
The chocolate-papers, tea-leaves, and, between

The rocks, the rusting soup-tins, till the first
Few families start the trek back to the cars.

The white steamer has gone. Like breathed-on glass
The sunlight has turned milky. If the worst
Of flawless weather is our falling short,
It may be that through habit these do best,
Coming to water clumsily undressed
Yearly; teaching their children by a sort
Of clowning; helping the old, too, as they ought.

Mountain Madness

John Collee

Before they built it 10 years ago, the Highest Hotel in the World must have seemed like a good idea. Situated on a ridge in the Himalayas, the Everest View is tastefully constructed in stone and natural wood. Those tourists who can afford a few hundred dollars for the weekend can fly in, stroll uphill from the airstrip and gaze out from their rooms at a picture-postcard view of the world's highest peak.

The hotel suffers, however, from a couple of practical drawbacks; the least of these being that it has no piped water, so that every drop has to be carried up by Sherpas. This would be almost justifiable if the place were a simple alpine *pensione* but the Everest View has baths and flush toilets. Knowing that the water in my loo cistern had been carried with great effort for a couple of miles uphill, I doubt if I could bring myself to pull the chain.

The other major problem is the hotel's very location – 13,000 feet above sea level, a height at which unacclimatized people are likely to succumb to altitude sickness. This is a strange condition in which a combination of low pressure and lack of oxygen causes fluid to accumulate in the lungs and tissues of the brain. In the mild form you develop a cough and headache and have difficulty sleeping, but the worst cases become rapidly and severely breathless, with mental confusion and loss of coordination. This can progress with frightening rapidity to coma and death.

The risk of altitude sickness increases with the speed of ascent – which is why professional Everest-climbers spend time getting acclimatized at lower altitudes rather than chartering a plane and flying direct to the Everest View. The hotel management confess that about 30 per cent of their guests will become ill after 24 hours there, which is probably a conservative estimate. To be fair, they do make some provision for this: altitude sickness can, to a degree, be prevented and treated with oxygen. The Everest View is the only hotel in the world I've found which provides it, as a matter of course, via room service. (The Sherpas on early Himalayan expeditions regarded oxygen as a magical restorative. They referred to it, reverentially, as 'English air'.)

In the past, most high-altitude mountaineers carried oxygen, but the fashion nowadays is for the fast, lightweight ascents. Such expeditions often leave the heavy oxygen cylinders behind, and a few seem to leave their common sense in the same rucksack. In a recent edition of *Wilderness Medicine* Dr Oswald Olez cites the Czechoslovakian expedition which, in 1988, attempted to climb Mount Everest equipped with the inner lining of one tent, two sleeping bags, two ropes and food for three days. Surprisingly, they reached the south summit where, less surprisingly, they all died. According to Dr Olez, of a total of 40 climbers who attempted Everest's summit that year, nine died, seven of them climbing without oxygen. The confusion and disorientation associated with altitude sickness probably played a large part in their deaths.

The standard drug treatment for altitude sickness includes the powerful drugs used to relieve lung congestion in severe heart failure. But the only definitive treatment is to get the sufferer back down the mountain as quickly as possible, into a normal atmosphere. An ingenious new treatment, based on this observa-tion, is the Gamow bag – a portable, pressurized tent, oper-ated by a foot pump, which can create a sea-level atmosphere around the victim. After a few hours in the Gamow bag, the victim has usually recovered suffi-ciently to manage the arduous descent.

On the same principle, maybe the only solution to the problems of the Everest View is to install airtight doors and windows and then pressurize the whole place like an aeroplane. This would of course confine the wealthy guests to spending most of their stay indoors but, reading the hotel's brochure, it seems that this is what the management already ex-pects.

Above an artist's impression of the hotel lounge it says: 'There are no planned activities at the Hotel Everest View yet many facilities are available to make your stay interesting and reward-ing. You can spend hours watching the ever-changing lighting and cloud formations on the moun-tains and watching great birds circling overhead. You can sit around the hotel's fireplace and discuss the day's happenings with other guests.'

I don't know how many hours' conversation the average million-aire businessman can get out of a day's changing cloud formations, but this particular quote from the brochure illuminates the hotel's central problem. The delight of being within sight of Everest is surely proportional to the time and effort you've spent in getting there. If you simply hopped on a private plane in Kathmandu you'll have a pretty superficial appreciation of the Everest region, and as a result you won't have much to talk about.

To my mind, to travel without sparing the time to assimilate is to defeat the purpose of going anywhere. Flying half-way up Mount Everest for a day to look at cloud formations through a Perspex oxygen mask seems to me symptomatic of a form of sickness which affects fast-lane tourism everywhere, and can only be relieved by a change of attitude.

Barracuda Breakfast

Kevin Pilley

Dress codes are usually fairly relaxed in American hotels but at the Emerald Lagoon in Key Largo, 54 miles south of Miami, they won't let you in even if you're not wearing a wetsuit, flippers and a snorkel. It is the world's first and only underwater hotel.

Everything in Florida involves large volumes of water – especially local beers. The southernmost state of the USA is the self-proclaimed water sports capital of the world and now, after all that snorkelling, water skiing, swimming with dolphins, hand-feeding moray eels, plus all those jetties, jacuzzis and glass-bottomed boat rides, you can even sleep the night in water if you want to.

Opened in 1986, the Jules Verne Lodge, sunk 30 ft. down in the Undersea Park close to the John Pennecamp Coral Reef Park and Key Largo Marine Sanctuary, can accommodate up to six in bunk-style accommodation in two bedrooms. Inside your 11 ft. by 50 ft. undersea sub-Atlantic habitat, formerly a marine research laboratory, you feel odd: as if you had

driven along the Interstate One in a large hi-tech caravan, your automatic coaster has suddenly malfunctioned and you have veered off the road through some palms and 'Tackle & Bait' ad hoardings and plunged into the sea only to land right way up on the sandy bottom. The Jules Verne underwater suite is more of a submerged caravan site than a hotel. But it is exclusive. Nobody bothers you for matches or sugar and the only Peeping Toms are barracudas.

Every window, 4 in. thick by 42 in. in diameter, offers a sea view. The Americans are keen to offer you 'limitless opportunities' and 'the ultimate', waking in the morning and drawing the curtain to see a four-foot barracuda staring at you is surely some kind of ultimate. Few Europeans get the chance to observe marine life so close. Likewise the colourful marine life make the most of the limitless opportunities of observing at close-range Europeans in their colourful Marks & Spencer's pyjamas.

When you check-in you need not show your passport, only a

diving certificate. If you haven't dived before you can attend a three-hour 'aquatic habitat orientation programme' which involves learning what salt water tastes like and how to put flippers on the right way. The secret of putting flippers on is that there is no secret. There is no right or wrong way to put on flippers. There is no such thing as left or right flipper. If you remember flippers go on your feet you can't go far wrong.

The programme is taken by the world's only full-time professional mermaid, Carla Rush, a 40-year-old from Illinois and former captain of a local dive charter boat.

She has been a 'pro' mermaid for nearly two years and will teach you how to operate your flippers, the rudiments of breathing compressed air, help you in and out of your wetsuit, clean your mask for you with her own spit, bring your meals, wash up, carry your bags and do anything else that needs doing, including pushing you in.

After a short downward swim you emerge up under the hotel into a dive port from where, once Carla has eased you out of your oxygen tank and towelled you down, you are shown to your living chambers. These are equipped with all mod cons. Carla then leaves you to your microwave filet mignon and lobster and returns to terra firma to man the control and wait on every whim. Room service is excellent and if you leave your shoes outside they are clean in the morning.

There isn't much to do underwater. Smoking and drinking are not allowed. But you can watch videos like John Wayne's *Hell Town* and, predictably, *Splash* and *20,000 Leagues Under The Sea*. You can hope that somebody rings you up. Wrong numbers are fun. You can ring anybody in the world. You may attempt to become a member of the Five Fathom Club or merely wonder how much air you have in your 600 square feet of living space.

The brochure boasts 'limitless' air supply as part of your package.

If lucky you might get a sighting of a manatee swimming past your dining room window. A manatee is a curious looking and very rare marine creature which can only be described as weighing 300 lbs, having the head of Bobby Charlton and body of a stout middle-aged woman.

When you check out you decompress. This ensures that you aren't suffering from 'the bends' – something your signature on your Visa and Mastercard can't prove – and receive your treasured Aquanaut certificate which verifies that you have spent the whole night in the sea and enjoyed all the benefits of the experience. These are obvious.

Staying underwater in Florida is the best way to avoid sunburn and mosquitos.

Perhaps the best thing about the Undersea Park is that it means you don't have to indulge in the ridiculous American ritual of sharing a sunset with a friend.

The Jules Verne Lodge, the Undersea Park, PO box 330 Key Largo, Florida 3303. Overnight hb tariff is $295 pp. Virgin Atlantic fly to Miami five times a week. Return prices range from £499–£599. Virgin Holidays offer special packages.

Coming Home

Reasons to be Cheerful

Frank Barrett

In 'DEPARTURES' recently I asked: When you return home after a holiday abroad, is there anything that makes you feel glad about getting back to Britain?

My question was inspired by *Down and out in Paris and London*, in which George Orwell reflects on the pleasures of Britain after travelling abroad: '. . . bathrooms, armchairs, mint sauce, new potatoes properly cooked, brown bread, marmalade, beer made with veritable hops . . . '

Letters have poured in from readers with their own lists of favourite things they miss when they are away. (To spare our blushes, I have omitted everyone's extremely fond feelings for the Saturday *Independent*.) For those of you settling back to workaday life after a summer trip abroad, here are some reasons to be cheerful...

Sylvia O'Leary, Norwich: English bacon; parks with grass that you are actually allowed to sit or lie on; red buses; paperboys;

'Bliss, after the relentless, exhausting heat of 'abroad', is the refreshing cool drizzle that meets us at the airport'

the milkman with the morning pinta; pub lunches; double cream; granary bread; and – oh bliss – after the relentless exhausting heat of 'abroad', the refreshing cool English drizzle that meets us at the airport.

Rachel Ives, Oxford: The sight of a game of cricket; scrupulous politeness – people who apologize for bumping into you when it was your fault; bus drivers who stop when you hail them even though you're not standing at a bus stop; pick-your own fruit farms; vegetarian food; the sheer joy of a hot day because they are so few and far between; ice-cream vans; manicured lawns and manageably sized insects; traffic islands and driving on the left; instant coffee; Earl Grey tea and chocolate digestives; sarcasm.

Kirti Joshi, Leicester: Hot mango pickle; Radio 3 cricket commentary; Channel 4 news; clever adverts and *Coronation Street*; variety of English accents; cynicism and humour; musty second-hand bookshops; winding B-roads; live music.

Sally Ingram, Shepperton: Flying into Gatwick and hearing from the seat behind an American voice saying: 'Are those real dandelions down there?'; windows without insect screens; the view of St Paul's from Hungerford footbridge; Marmite; public toilets (because the doors go down to the floor); hedgerows; London parks; oak trees; the shipping forecast on Radio 4.

Mrs R. Haigh, Louth: British twilight; unarmed policemen; raspberries, gooseberries, apples; proper bread, biscuits and cheese.

Frances Tompkins, London SE10: Primroses; hawthorn flowers; children singing; swifts at twilight and a good cup of tea.

Beverly Orton, London NW6: Marmite; live broadcasts from the House of Commons; leafy parks in London; bacon sandwiches; our special humour; our marvellous theatre; Boots the Chemist; our gardens; churches ... goodness knows why I'm always trying to leave this green and once pleasant land.

Pamela Jeffreys, Muswell Hill, London: Cream teas; steak and kidney pie; gooseberries; broad beans; sausages and bacon; large flat mushrooms; potted shrimps; pork and egg pie; steamed syrup puddings; cottage gardens; stately homes; the National Trust; Ramblers Association; public libraries; non-vocational adult education classes and English newspapers.

Susan Downs, Bradford: Fat Friesian cows and limestone walls; bacon and eggs and large cream teas; green, green fields and carpets of heather; the congenial togetherness in pubs with wet clothes drying around the fire; the comforting chink of milk bottles being put on the doorstep by the milkman; and the shipping forecast – knowing you are safe with all this weather going on around you.

Bridget Crowson, Isle of Wight: Walking the dog in total comfort in fine drizzle while wearing an old Barbour and not meeting another soul.

Audrey Dingle, Cheltenham: Water freely available in restaurants; cars stop at zebra crossings; well-mannered adults and children; a cup of tea, piece of toast and our bed.

Mrs F. Waddell, Clacton: Roast beef and Yorkshire pudding; fish and chips; Radio 3 all day; my own bathroom; full English breakfast; Essex roses;

green, green grass and lots of trees.

Rosalind A. Edwards, St Albans: Hanging baskets; pick-your-own strawberries and raspberries; cheddar cheese with real rind; the tinkle of milk bottles as the milkman delivers and the funny whine of his float as he drives off; understanding other people's conversations; the rustle and plop of newspapers and post through the letter box. And for her husband: Radio 4; marmalade and mint.

Mrs Dorothy Steward, Edinburgh: A decent *Scottish* black pudding for Sunday morning. Bliss!!

Wayne Warren, Broadstairs: The green colour of trees and grass – and the sharp evening light after a storm.

Elizabeth Stamp, Oxford: A cup of tea made with boiling water and the milk waiting on the doorstep; the uncertainty of British weather and the brave Met Office forecasts; the privacy and space of the London park; the British bicycle with no threatening brake on the back pedal; choral evensong and that superb English choral sound; breakfast with the *Today* programme; marmalade and *The Independent*.

Tom Baldwin, Darlington: Zebra crossings where motorists stop of their own accord; public toilets where you may leave without a sour-faced woman glaring at you for change; the Great British queue.

Rosemary Emmett, Christchurch: Daily milk; queues at bus stops; over-the-counter remedies at chemists; pretty gardens; the rural footpath system; dogs and cats being treated with love and respect; church bells; parking in either direction; tea made in a pot and accompanied by a jug of milk.

Sheila Podmore, Brentwood: I am wheelchair-bound and am grateful for the profusion of dropped kerbstones throughout towns in the UK, and most places of interest are made accessible by the use of ramps and other devices to enable mobility – the National Trust in particular has made many of its foothpaths negotiable by wheelchair.

Eileen Hills, Marbella: Smoked mackerel; Stilton; Dundee cake; gooseberries; red and black currants; daffodils; the trees in Sussex in May.

Adrian Skelton, Birmingham: a broadsheet newspaper; Marmite; digestive biscuits; a frosty morning; an English apple.

Lorna Day, Aberdeen: clean, unsmelly toilets; toilet paper in toilets; crush-free buses; orderly queuing; real fruit juice; colourful gardens; British Rail; pedestrian-conscious traffic; Brian Redhead.

Eileen Miller, Huntingdon: English eating apples; Jordan's four-grain muesli and organic oats; green Oxo cubes; the superb public library service; Radios 3, 4 and 5; all the TV channels; Asda and the Body Shop; glorious unpredictable weather.

'Wheelchair-bound, I am grateful for the profusion of dropped kerbstones throughout the UK, and ramps and other devices'

Brenda Buck, Leeds: my own pillow; our back garden; the BBC (particularly Radio 4); Test matches and the Test grounds; visiting National Trust properties; my own home-made date spread on hot buttered wholemeal toast.

Edna Barron, Highgate: Mature cheddar cheese; Dundee cake; little gem lettuces; milk and papers delivered daily; being able to cross roads safely on crossings.

Bee Mortimer, St Albans: The salt-of-the-earth people; their humour; real salted butter; not having to explain.

Diana Miller, Cheltenham: English puddings; ploughman's lunches; apples; paperboys; milkmen; TV; cream teas; lollipop ladies; the NHS and ambulance service; St John Ambulance Brigade and Relate; fish and chip shops; garden centres; ice-cream vans; libraries; evening classes; Open University courses.

Constance Clark, Falmouth: A shower controllable for heat and volume; Cranks sunflower bread; Earl Grey tea; sunlight filtering through the bedroom curtains at dawn.

And many, many more...

Wherever I Hang

Grace Nichols

I leave me people, me land, me home
For reasons, I not too sure
I forsake de sun
And de humming-bird splendour
Had big rats in de floorboard
So I pick up me new-world-self
And come, to this place call England
At first I feeling like I in dream —
De misty greyness
I touching de walls to see if they real
They solid to de seam
And de people pouring from de underground system
Like beans
And when I look up to de sky
I see Lord Nelson high – too high to lie

And is so I sending home photos of myself
Among de pigeons and de snow
And is so I warding off de cold
And is so, little by little
I begin to change my calypso ways
Never visiting nobody
Before giving them clear warning
And waiting me turn in queue

Now, after all this time
I get accustom to de English life
But I still miss back-home side
to tell you de truth
I don't know really where I belaang

   Yes, divided to de ocean
   Divided to de bone

Wherever I hang me knickers – that's my home.

My Favourite Places

Yehudi Menuhin

One of the most magical places I've ever been to is Ninfa, south of Rome, between the mountains and the sea. I don't know what's happened to it now; it was the property of an English family. It has been a holy site for thousands of years. A stream of very fast cool water ran down the mountain there, making its way to the sea, and the area of beautifully-watered land in the middle of what is probably not very good land gave it a quality which people came to revere. They built their temples, they built their churches, and the gardens have in the meantime overgrown all these temples and churches.

That atmosphere of a place that has been sacred for 3,000 years is something difficult to find. Today's world doesn't respect anything: neither trees nor sacred areas. It just goes roughshod over everything.

We spend our holidays on a Greek island and that has changed completely over 30 years. There used to be five broken-down taxis and no tourists – my wife makes a distinction between tourists and travellers. Travellers were mostly archaeologists, professors, students, who came because they were interested in Greek history. Now they come for the sun and the beaches. They're young, full of energy and delightful but the sheer numbers have changed.

The whole quality of life has changed because with 300,000 tourists and an island with a population of 8,000, everyone is very, very rich, or most people are. The land goes up in value and people's values change from knitting to jewellery shops, and from selling local fish to dress shops. The streets used to be so clean. Today they're too busy.

Things change. As a boy I loved the sheer space of America, the idea of thousands of miles of mountains and deserts. Now, in my old age, I like snugness and even little places, such lovely ones in England, without a view, just around a stream, or a mill, in some idyllic cove.

That may be one reason why I love my house in London, because it has everything. It has the view from the top floor and I can see the sun rise and set and in its whole southern orbit, and there are also rooms where one is snug. If you create your own atmosphere in your home then this becomes the favourite place.

Sir Yehudi Menuhin is a violinist and conductor, and founder of the Yehudi Menuhin School.

Beyond Forbidden Frontiers

Nick Danziger

Making an excursion through Tibet, Nick Danziger is greeted with warm hospitality and some unusual regional delicacies.

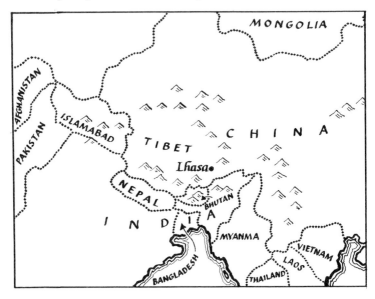

Our diet on this side trip was limited. Normally, I would happily eat dry raw yak meat, but on one occasion I hesitated. In fact, my stomach turned, for I was offered some really ancient meat covered with a patina of dust and grime. It looked as if it had been festering in a cupboard for years.

'How old might this be?' I asked tactfully, as one enquiring about the vintage of a wine.

The question pleased the Tibetan. '1983,' he said proudly.

'1983?!' Horrified.

'November.' A true connoisseur.

There was no answer to that. I ate it. I must admit that it tasted just like what it was – vintage, raw yak meat. Dried. I felt that it was even a good year, and a good month.

More often than not food was scarce, and we came to rely on our skin pouches to mix tsamba in. We grew adept at mixing the right amounts of tea and flour, and the dough eggs we lived on we found surprisingly nutritious and even tasty. But food wasn't the only thing that was scarce. There wasn't a lot of accommodation either. If we arrived at a village, we were totally dependent on the kindness of the villagers, for we had nothing to barter. Many at first mistook us for the local travelling salesmen, who go from village to village with their wares, but we encountered great generosity, once the misapprehension had been overcome. We had to repay this somehow and once when we stayed with a family for four days and they refused payment, Dave gave them our supply of butter – something they could ill afford. The butter was welcome to them, as they were very poor, but they smeared the teacups' rims with it generously, as custom requires.

Climbing one valley wall, we came across some hot springs. We were bashful about bathing in them in front of the village women, but the men pointed out with a grin that the ladies had seen all that sort of stuff before. I had noticed that in Lhasa the general view foreigners held of Tibetans was that they were filthy. But in the capital there is little water available for the luxury of washing as the land is frozen hard for most of the year, whereas here, where water is plentiful, Tibetans are as clean as most westerners, and cleaner than many I've known.

If my appearance was one of respectability for most, it nevertheless frightened babies into tears (most Tibetans are beardless or, like Mongolians, have sparse facial hair). Children were curious but cautious. When I extended my hand in friendship they were puzzled at first, but once one nervously took the initiative and shook my hand, the action gave rise to general merriment – so much so that sometimes the handshaking became a game: who could shake my hand hardest and longest. To cement the new friendship, I would do my Charlie Chaplin impersonations for them. Or I'd be an angry old man and pull faces. Some of the children took to us so much that they insisted on accompanying us on excursions. Four delightful such companions were Mimo, Mima, Putsch and Auto, who waited for us to appear every morning that we stayed in their village. Leading us, they showed us shortcuts that we'd never have found by ourselves. And if it sometimes involved walking through the middle of military barracks, the soldiers never seemed to mind.

Handshaking was one thing, but in some areas older traditions persisted. As a token of respect you have to stick your tongue out in greeting. I never quite got used to this...

Back home, Danziger is haunted by his memories of his travels and disturbed by news of fighting which has broken out in Afghanistan, where he spent part of his journey.

...On my return to England I led a monastic existence, working non-stop on this book except for two short breaks. Penniless, I returned to my parents' home to live, although I felt something of a burden to them. However I found my return home was as unsettling as travelling, as the apparent security of the English countryside contrasted vividly with the 'flood' of memories of the journey which pass before my eyes as I write. Although my convictions remain intact, I find myself caught between two worlds: I have become a stranger to my previous world but at the same time remain an outsider in those countries which I journeyed through.

I spent a lot of time with my former girl-friend Noo. I was restless, and discontented, but I took comfort in Noo's company. She is one of the few people who can understand my predicament, perhaps because she has shared one journey with me, and because her experiences of life are similar to my own. For others, I must sometimes make life difficult. It's hard for me to sit down to Sunday lunch, at table, with the place settings neatly laid. And now, even more than in the past, I find it hard to join in the agreeable small-talk of dinner table conversation. But I am lucky in my surroundings. My parents live deep in the Wiltshire countryside and my bedroom overlooks rolling hills. Here, I swim, I walk, and I write.

There are the occasional unnerving moments. The first sound of a helicopter or a jet causes my heart to miss a beat. The thumping sound of rotor blades brings all the horrors of Afghanistan flooding back. I think the greatest shock was going out jogging at dawn once. Again an image was stirred by the sound of a jet overhead. Half of Britain was asleep, and yet in Hauze Kerbas everyone would be out in the dirt road waiting, waiting for the first bombing raid.

The journey brought me many friends, and still now, a year and more since my return, I correspond with many of them. I receive news from mujahedeen, they are waiting for a copy of the book; and the last I heard of Ismail Khan, several hundred of his mujahedeen remain besieged in Hauze Kerbas surrounded by 20,000 Afghan government and Soviet soldiers.

Perhaps that is not my battle any more. I want to return to painting; I want to discuss work with art students; and I want to explore the great possibilities that I have become aware of in writing. There is a part of me that would like to try acting; and there is certainly a part of me that would like to travel again. The vast world is forever calling.

Why have I said all this? Probably just to set the record straight. I have yet to feel any sense of accomplishment. The most important thing for me is the knowledge that I have tried my best, and attempted to stick to my principles and retain my integrity. What I brought back, and what I want to communicate, is the greatest reward travel can give you: understanding. I got home shortly after there had been severe riots in Birmingham. But the rioters had much in common with many of the people I had met in the Third World. People with a stake in society, with property, don't riot. It is those who have nothing that do, and they do so not out of envy, or irresponsibility, but out of frustration. Revolution is born of a poverty which does not allow the sharing of material wealth. My journey has taught me that there can be misery and deprivation in the most beautiful of settings. I hope that now I can see beyond what is picturesque to deeper understanding. And my journey has taught me something else: that we are all the same under the skin, and under the sun.

Sadly, even the superficial differences between us that make travel worthwhile are disappearing in the face of western cultural domination. I won my Fellowship to follow ancient trade routes. The rich variety and colour of life along those routes continues – but only just. And it will go under forever unless the nations of the east can compete on equal terms not only in trade, but in ideas. Why should they think that what comes from the west is automatically best? Why should they ape us rather than be true to their own values? I arrived in Southampton on 10 September 1985, dressed in my Afghan clothes. The crew of the *Kowloon Bay* had told me that I'd find things difficult dressed as I was, but I hadn't taken them seriously. They'd ordered a taxi to take me from the dock to the station. The cabbie neglected to put his meter on, until I asked him to in a broad cockney accent which made him jump. Then he was all apologies.

The train journey wasn't a problem. In fact, it was even comfortable, because although my carriage was crowded I was left alone with four empty seats around me – and it wasn't as if I hadn't made full use of my bathroom aboard the *Kowloon Bay*. In London, however, things really began to tighten up. Not one taxi stopped for me, so that in the end I was obliged to go to my stepfather's place of work and get him to flag one down.

'Why won't anyone stop for me?' I asked the cabbie as soon as we'd set off.

'Can't be too careful these days, mate.'

'Would you have stopped for me if I'd been alone?'

'Yes, but then I recognize your costume. I was in Afghanistan in the sixties. Got any smoke?' It was a question I was asked many times.

I suppose I ought to have abandoned my Afghan clothes, but I found wearing them in London most educational. Everywhere I went I was either shunned or regarded with undisguised suspicion. But the biggest shock came on my second day back. I was walking down an empty John Islip Street in Westminster when suddenly I heard the sound of a van approaching me from behind. I knew it was a van because I used to drive one and the engine has an unmistakable sound. It slowed slightly as it drew level with me. A red Post Office van. The man in the passenger seat was sliding his door open. He was looking at me. The look wasn't friendly.

'You f.....g nignog,' he yelled. Then the van sped off.

I was home.

Postscript

Frank Kusy

Off the plane back in Heathrow, I did not – unlike Kevin – have a plateful of cheese sandwiches waiting for me in the airport lounge. Instead, I returned straight home and ate a simple meal of rice and yoghourt – the nearest thing to an Indian 'thali' I could find.

Then I ran a bath, my first in four months, and discovered on the scales that I was two whole stones lighter than when I had left England. Finally, I climbed into bed, faintly aware of the deafening silence in the streets outside, and slept for the whole day.

I woke up feeling like I had been wrung through a mangle backwards. Then, as consciousness returned, I found myself thinking of my next journey. Where would I be going? Why, back to India of course.

Most people do.

Activities

The Art of Travel

Background notes

Jack Shamash's article, *Mindless in Gaza*, questions the purpose of travel, as part of a weekly 'Reputations' feature in *The Guardian* newspaper which challenges accepted values and assumptions. *Around the World in Eighty Days* is a novel by Jules Verne, written in 1872, in which Phileas Fogg and his faithful servant, Passepartout, take up a challenge to travel around the world in only eighty days. Their journey is made for real more than a century later by Michael Palin and his own Passepartout – a film crew of five people.

Emigrants hoping to begin new lives in a new world often travelled to America by sea, looking out for the welcoming Statue of Liberty as they approached Manhattan Island. Jonathan Raban's book *Hunting Mr Heartbreak* retraces their passage across the Atlantic during bad weather.

Freya Stark is a remarkable adventurer who, from 1928 onwards, has travelled constantly. This extract from *A Winter in Arabia* describes her descent by plane to begin a journey into a previously unexplored region of Arabia.

Mindless in Gaza

Group work

1   Before reading Jack Shamash's article, look at these statements about travel. Discuss what you think each one means. Which do you most agree/most strongly disagree with?

☐   Travel opens your mind; it lets you see the world and learn about other people, other places.

☐   Most travel is actually tourism: everything is decided for you – how to get there, where to stay, what to eat, where to visit. It's all pre-packaged, artificial and lifeless.

☐   To be a traveller rather than a tourist you have to travel alone.

☐ Real travelling involves risks and decisions; real travelling can happen within a mile of your own home.

☐ We travel in order to come home: having travelled, we know ourselves better.

2 Now read the article. Which of these words best describes the writer's attitude to travel: *hostile, cynical, probably right, probably wrong, witty*? In your opinion, which of the statements in question 1 best applies to the writer's views?

3 Make a list in two columns to show the advantages and disadvantages of travel. Start by looking again at Jack Shamash's views: what are his specific complaints about travel? Then think carefully about the advantages you would place against his disadvantages. Make your list as full as possible.

Written assignment

Write a response to Jack Shamash's article, stating the positive aspects of travel, but accepting that there are also drawbacks to travelling. You could refer to other pieces of travel writing that you have already read in this collection. Make your written response about the same length as Shamash's – approximately 500 words.

Around the World in Eighty Days (1872)

Pair work

1 Looking at the content and style of the extract, how can you tell that:

a) it is set in the past?

b) it refers to upper-class people?

Make two lists for your answers.

2 The extract is fictional rather than factual – Phileas Fogg does not really exist. But how does the writer, Jules Vernes, try to convince us that the events portrayed are real? Make a note of the details from this extract that give it this realism.

3 Look again at the reaction of the passengers to the Sioux Indians. Look at the words used to describe the Indians. How does Jules Verne try to ensure that we feel sympathetic to the white passengers and hostile to the American Indians? How does this reflect attitudes towards American Indians in the late Nineteenth century?

Written assignment

Many stories, novels and films use journeys to provide their structure – think of *Murder on the Orient Express* or the 'disaster' movies of the

1970s. Use a boat, an aeroplane, or a train journey as the setting for a story of your own. It might be a mystery, a romance, a comedy or a thriller. Try to build in the detail of travelling and the journey as well as a strong story-line.

Around the World in Eighty Days (1988)

Pair work

1 On his train-journey across the American West, Michael Palin says of the passengers, 'I get the feeling these are not average Americans. They're people who care about their environment.' What does he mean? Are there any other negative references about the USA in the extract?

2 If you placed a paragraph from Verne's book against a paragraph from Palin's, would you be able to tell that one is fictional and one is factual? Try it out: choose two paragraphs at random from the descriptions of the ride into Utah. What clues are there, in the language and the detail, about whether the journeys are real or invented?

Group work

Look at Michael Palin's list of essential items for travelling around the world on pages 13–14. Decide on the items you would find it essential to take for this journey? As a group, make a final list of the items you would pack.

Written assignments

1 In the second part of the extract, Palin describes the people and places he sees as he travels by train across America. Choose an ordinary journey – perhaps a bus ride to school – and try to capture the flavour of the journey in a piece of descriptive writing. Pay particular attention to the sights and sounds of the people around you.

2 Using the work you have done on the style, language and attitudes of each extract, write a comparison of Verne's style and Palin's. You could use these three features of their writing along with actual content and humour as the paragraph headings for your piece.

Hunting Mr Heartbreak

Pair work

1 How does Raban build up the effect of the storm's approach? Look at the way he uses the reactions of his fellow passengers, the motion of the ship, the weather reports. Discuss the way that the description is built up.

2   Raban talks of 'a characteristically Jacksonian description' (see page 23). Find some other examples of the way the Captain understates the effects of the storm.

3   For some people the greatest idea of luxury is to take a cruise, to spend months on board a cruise liner enjoying sunshine, excellent food and drink, away from the worries of everyday life. Other people think it sounds awful – cooped up on a ship, at the mercy of the sea, surrounded by people whom you might not like. What is your viewpoint?

Group work

Imagine you are a group of passengers on board ship during bad weather. You are attempting to eat dinner at the Captain's table. Ignorantly, one of your party comments that the motion of the ship must be caused by poor piloting and complains to the Captain. In your groups role play the discussion that follows.

Written assignments

1   Imagining yourself as a passenger on the *Conveyor*, write a diary of events describing the build-up of the storm. Focus on your own reaction and those of the other passengers.

2   In the role of a passenger who has experienced bad weather at sea, after spending a good deal of money on your luxury cruise, write a letter to the Managing Director of Albatross Cruises, describing your experiences and attempting to obtain a refund.

A Winter in Arabia

Pair work

1   How can you tell that the writer is excited to be returning to Arabia? Pick out some key words that show this.

2   What clues are there in the passage that the extract was written in the past? Discuss any evidence you can find.

Group work

Choose three paragraphs from the extract and select an appropriate piece of music to play in the background. Try reading the passage to different pieces of music. What effect does the music have? Does it *add* to the effect of the words, or distract the listener's attention?

Written assignments

1   Rewrite one paragraph of Stark's work, removing all the adjectives and adverbs. Then write a paragraph describing the effect this has.
2   You have been asked to reduce Stark's journal to 98 words for a leisure magazine. You cannot add any of your own words. As you edit down the article, try to produce a summary which keeps the main details and the atmosphere of the original.

Explorers

Background notes

Eric Newby is a well-known travel writer and former travel editor of the *Observer* newspaper. In *Travels in Harrods* he recalls as a child exploring Harrods, London's most famous department store, with his mother and nurse. Christina Dodwell sets off to travel in Iran and Turkey on horseback. In the extract she climbs Mount Ararat in search of the remains of Noah's Ark.

Julian Barnes is famous for his brilliantly funny novels. In this extract from *A History of the World in 10½ Chapters* he looks at the Noah legend from a different angle – from the viewpoint of one of the animal passengers on the Ark whose identity does not become clear until the final sentence of the novel.

Isabella Bird left her life as the daughter of a Victorian country parson and turned explorer. In this extract she climbs with a small team led by 'Jim', high up the Rocky Mountains of America.

Charles Hose's explorations focus on the amazing natural life-forms noted during his journey through Borneo. Redmond O'Hanlon also travels through Borneo, but his impressions of the wildlife, described in *Into the Heart of Borneo*, are much less pleasant. In contrast, Annie Dillard's essay presents her much more positive impressions of living in the jungle.

Travels in Harrods

Pair work

1   Make a list of the different elements in Harrods which Eric Newby likes and dislikes. What, if anything, do the 'dislikes' have in common?
2   Pick out three sentences which particularly make the atmosphere of Newby's Harrods come to life. Discuss why they have this effect.

Group work

1 Talk about your own memories of being taken shopping when you were a small child. Which shops did you enjoy visiting? Which did you loathe? Think about why you reacted as you did.

2 Eric Newby's article has been placed in the 'Explorers' section. Treat the text as if it is the report of a traveller to some exotic new world (which, in a way, it is). Using Newby's account as a starting-point, write a scripted report for a radio travel programme in which you are a team of explorers in Harrods. Each explorer describes a different department. Your script might begin with these ideas:

Explorer 1: Ahead of me, I see a sign saying 'Restaurant'. It's not clear from where I am hiding, at the door of the Ladies' Retiring Room, what might be waiting for me inside. Certainly there are sounds of clatterings and conversations. I'm going in to find out more...

Written assignment

Choose a shop which has particularly strong associations for you – a supermarket where your parents always took you or the local corner shop. You could try bringing the place to life through words, describing its sight, sounds and smells, and focusing on one particular visit you remember making. Or you could structure your writing as Eric Newby does, using different parts of the store to write about different memories.

A Traveller on Horseback

Pair work

1 'I liked the idea of looking for Noah's Ark.'... 'Personally I didn't expect to find the Ark, but that didn't stop me from looking.' What do you think was Christina Dodwell's motivation in searching for the Ark? Look at these statements and say which you most agree with.

☐ Finding the Ark is unimportant to her; it's the journey which counts.

☐ She is driven by curiosity – so much evidence exists about the Ark that she wants to find out the truth for herself.

☐ It is impossible to say, based simply on her account, what motivates her.

2 How do you feel about the ending of Dodwell's journey up Mount Ararat – disappointed that she does not continue? Or satisfied with her explanation for not doing so?

Group work

'Goals are like destinations, they don't always matter. Our journey was enough in itself'. What do you think Dodwell means in her conclusion? Talk about occasions when you have failed to achieve what you had hoped and discuss what your feelings were.

Written assignment

Is Dodwell's wish to travel across Turkey and Iran on horseback admirable or reckless? Imagine an unusual, and perhaps dangerous, form of travel you would like to experience and describe what the attractions are.

A History of the World in 10½ Chapters

Pair work

1   Which one of these words do you think best describes Julian Barnes' version of the Bible story: *irreverent*, *far-fetched*, *modern*, *witty*? Explain your choice.
2   How would you describe the character of Noah as presented in the passage? How soon do you realize that Noah is not being described by a human narrator?
3   What creature do you imagine is narrating the story? Are there any clues?

Group work

Some people would argue that Julian Barnes's version of the Bible story is blasphemous, encouraging us to laugh at both the Bible and God. Others would say that it's simply a humorous piece filling in details left out in the Bible version, but not attacking the Bible story in any way. What do the members of your group think?

Written assignment

Take a legend or fairytale and rewrite it from the point of view of one of the other characters, e.g. Baby Bear from *Goldilocks and the Three Bears* describing what it was like to find that an intruder had broken in and eaten your porridge. Aim to make the style light and amusing like the narrator's voice in Barnes' piece.

A Lady's Life in the Rocky Mountains

Pair work

1 How can you tell, from the language, that this extract was written last century? What clues are there? Make a note of any words or phrases that show this.

2 What are the various dangers that Isabella Bird encounters during the climb? How would you describe her attitude to them?

3 Which one of these words do you think best describes Bird's written style: *poetic*, *nervous*, *awed*, *objective*? Explain your choice.

Written assignments

1 Produce a newspaper front-page announcing the successful ascent of Pike's Peak by Isabella Bird. Model your page on a present-day newspaper format and think about the main focus of your story. For example, how would a tabloid newspaper, like *Today* or *The Daily Mirror*, treat the fact that she is a woman? Would it be right to emphasize her sex, or should the story concentrate purely on her achievement? Whichever type of story you choose, take care to phrase your headline and tell Bird's story in an authentic newspaper style.

2 Write Jim's version of the day's climb. You might include his comments on how Isabella deals with the challenge and the story of his 'great sorrow' that led him to a life as a mountain guide.

All on the Bornean Shore

Group work

1 Hose's descriptions are of the wildlife of a foreign land rather than of a journey or a place. Do you feel that such an extract is suitable for a book of travel writing? How does it add to and reflect on the O'Hanlon and Dillard pieces that follow it?

2 What features of Hose's written style create its objective, scientific tone? Pick out appropriate words and phrases that show this.

Written assignment

Undertake some research into famous explorers or naturalists. Focus on one in particular and, drawing upon reference books, but writing in your own words, give an account of his or her achievements.

Into the Heart of Borneo

Pair work

1   O'Hanlon writes very powerfully about the non-human inhabitants in the jungle. How much of an explorer are you? Would you want to travel to the places he describes?
2   Look at O'Hanlon's description of the leeches. Which one of these words and phrases best describes the style of his description: *unconcerned, seemingly unconcerned but panicky underneath, fascinated, scientific*? Explain your choice.

Written assignment

Use O'Hanlon's description as a starting point to put together a small A5 pamphlet entitled, 'Some hazards when travelling'. Try consulting a medical dictionary, travel guides and other reference books to research some of the dangers likely to be encountered on jungle expeditions, and give possible remedies.

In the Jungle

Pair work

1   Annie Dillard begins by calling the Napo River an 'out-of-the-way place'. She concludes by describing it as 'in the way'. Discuss what she means and how she shows in her account the reasons why her view has changed.
2   How does Dillard portray the native population of the Napo River area? Find examples in the text of how her open attitude towards the Indians helps her learn more about their life-style.
3   Devise an interview with Annie Dillard to discuss what she has learnt from her time in the jungle. Between you, think up a series of ten questions to ask her. Then role play the interview and, if possible, record it.

Group work

Compare Hose's, O'Hanlon's and Dillard's accounts of the life in the jungle. Which gives the harshest impression of conditions? Which extract did you find most interesting and why? How do the writers' written styles and approaches differ?

Written assignment

Write a comparison of Annie Dillard's description of the jungle and those of Redmon O'Hanlon and Charles Hose. Look at the different responses to their surroundings that each writer conveys? Which do you prefer and why? You might write your comparison in the style of a book review. Start by studying one such review, perhaps from a Sunday newspaper. Look at how the reviewer introduces each book and links comments on them. How does he or she indicate how good the book is?

Travellers

Background notes

Robyn Davidson's book, *Tracks*, describes her fulfilment of an unusual ambition – to travel across the Australian desert with camels. Mark Shand, in his more recent book *Travels on my Elephant*, overcomes his sense of restlessness by travelling through India on Tara the elephant.

Smita Patel, a British Asian woman, travels through India with her boy-friend and is subjected to considerable racial harassment. Well-known travel writer Colin Thubron describes his anxiety at travelling in a car through Russia in the days before the iron curtain was lifted.

In *Sequins for a Ragged Hem*, Amryl Johnson retraces her roots to Trinidad, rediscovering its excitement and exotic customs. In his article from the *Independent*, Greg Ward intentionally avoids the tourist clichés of Hawaii and courts a more dangerous, unexpected side of the Big Island.

Tracks

Group work

1   What facts did you already know about camels before reading Robyn Davidson's account? What facts have you learnt from the extract? Make a list.
2   Davidson herself calls her idea 'lunatic'. What clues are there in the account about why she undertakes her journey in the first place?

Written assignment

You have been asked to write a journalist's account of Davidson's journey in just 400 words. Which aspects of the extract will you focus upon and which will you cut?

Choose the particular newspaper that you will write for and examine the style of one of its 'features' articles (rather than a 'news' item). How long are the sentences and paragraphs? What kind of vocabulary is used? Does the writer avoid saying 'I' or is it written in a quite personal style? Write a paragraph at the end of your report discussing what you chose to include and omit.

Travels on My Elephant

Pair work

1   What do you know about elephants? Do some research. An especially good source of information is Heathcote Williams' poem, *Sacred Elephant*.
2   The extract finishes with Mark Shand's comment that Tara changes him. How does his outlook on life change in these few pages?
3   Like a number of writers in this book, Mark Shand has a taste for adventure: riding elephants or camels, climbing mountains. Are these heroic or crazy schemes? Discuss the type of adventure you would like to pursue, given time and money.

Group work

Compare Davidson's account of her journey by camel to Shand's description of travelling by elephant. How do the two writers' styles differ? Which extract appeals to you more? Discuss why.

Written assignments

1   Use your research into the behaviour and characteristics of elephants. Write an account for the non-specialist reader introducing your findings.
2   When Mark Shand leaves India, Tara stays behind. Although he knows that she will be well looked-after, Shand finds the parting upsetting. Many of us have similar feelings at the end of holidays, sometimes because of friends we have made and must leave. Think of a time you experienced these feelings and write about them in a personal essay.

Between Two Cultures

Pair work

1   List the ways in which Smita Patel is treated differently from her boy-friend. How many of these are linked:
a)   to her gender

b) her race?

2   Discuss what Patel means when she says: 'It was mortifying when I realized that I was dismissing part of my own culture in a way that can only be described as racist'.

Group work

Travel writing is often concerned with how we cope with being an outsider in a different community. Some pieces show a writer's success at integrating into a new culture; others show feelings of exclusion.

On your own, look back through some of the extracts included in this collection. List two which show the writer never managing to integrate; two which show success at becoming a part of the society. Compare and discuss your choices. Which type of travel writing makes the more interesting reading?

Written assignment

Think of a time when you have felt an outsider, either abroad, or within a group of people nearer to home. Describe in detail your feelings, the attempts you made to become accepted, and the success or failure of these attempts.

Among the Russians

Pair work

1   Thubron begins by recognizing his own early lack of knowledge about Russia. How much do you know about this vast country? Before reading the extract, make your own list of 'Facts about Russia', putting a tick against those you are certain of and a question mark against those which you are uncertain about.

2   After reading Thubron's account, what have you learnt about Russia? Make another list alongside your first one.

3   Do you think that the extract actually contains too much factual information? Does Thubron's extremely detailed style help or hinder you in picturing the scenes he describes?

Written assignment

Thubron writes about the power of the Russian landscape. Think of a place which has had a strong effect on you – an unfamiliar city, a barren moor, a deep forest. Write a personal essay contrasting two of these and discussing why they have this effect upon you.

Sequins for a Ragged Hem

Pair work

1 Looking particularly at the dialogue and vocabulary, discuss how Amryl Johnson makes her description of Trinidad vivid.
2 Amryl Johnson describes the crab racing without revealing much of what she feels about it. Would your description of events differ from hers? Discuss whether you think the sport is cruel.

Group work

1 Often when abroad we see customs with which we might not agree. Discuss this dilemma.
  You are on holiday in Spain. A friend has bought expensive tickets to see a bullfight this evening. You hate the idea of bullfighting, knowing how cruel it is and how the bulls are humiliated. On the other hand, you don't want to ruin the relationship with your friend – especially as you have another 10 days of the holiday left. What do you do?
2 Think of other moral dilemmas which might occur on holiday, and make a note of them. Then pool the dilemmas in your groups.

Written assignment

Take some of the moral dilemmas written by others in your group. Copy one out and, beneath it, write a paragraph answer. Then move on to the next dilemma and write your answer to that. Finally compare what you have written with others in the group, and discuss the different responses that emerge.

When Pele Blows, The Lava Flows

Pair work

1 When you think about the island of Hawaii, what images come to mind? Where have you gained these impressions of the place – through visits, friends' visits, through television, films, or books? Why do you think so many of us know so much about some islands which are so small?
2 Look at the first three paragraphs again. Which of these statements best describes the author's attitude to the changes that have taken place

on Hawaii over the past two hundred years? Discuss your choice with a partner, picking sentences out of the article to support your opinion.

☐ The author thinks that what has happened is wrong but accepts that we can't do anything about it.

☐ He wishes the island had remained unspoilt.

☐ He sees that Hawaii has been ruined by tourism but still possesses positive features.

3 What questions would you like to ask Greg Ward about Hawaii which you feel are not answered in his article?

Written assignment

The article shows two sides of Hawaii: one appeals to tourists, the other to travellers. Refer to some real holiday brochure or advertisements and produce two adverts to attract visitors to a place you know – perhaps your home town. One should appeal to tourists, the other to travellers. Which features of the place, if any, will you mention in both pages? Concentrate more on the text of your adverts than their overall design. How will the wording differ according to the two different audiences?

Tourists

Background notes

The humourist, Keith Waterhouse, opens this section with a tongue-in-cheek look at the language of travel brochures. Some extracts from examples of actual advertisements from magazines/newspapers follow on from this.

In his *Postcard from Epcot*, Clive James casts a cynical eye over one of the Disney worlds.

'Betjemanesque' is a Simon Rae poem based on the work of an earlier poet, John Betjeman. It takes Betjeman's eye for social detail and applies it to features of modern popular travel.

Philip Larkin's poem looks back to an earlier age, when holidays at British resorts were the annual family treat. His poem examines the British at play, focusing on their slight reserve and their retained sense of family responsibility.

The section ends with a look at two unusual hotels: one overlooking Everest, described in John Collee's *Observer* column; the other by Kevin Pilley describing an underwater hotel in Florida.

How to Speak Brochurese

Pair work

1 From your own/your family's experience, think of some more examples to add to Waterhouse's Dictionary of Brochurese, and make a note of them.

2 Imagine you are a tourist at a hotel and you have been misled by the details in the brochure. Role play the scene in which you complain to the manager about the gap between the description given in the brochure and the reality.

Written assignments

1 Put together a class collection of recent holiday brochures. Select one particularly 'vivid' brochure entry and using Waterhouse's 'Brochurese Dictionary', write a 'translation' of the entry to give the 'real' picture of the holiday, hotel, scenery, etc.

2 Using words and phrases like those listed in Waterhouse's 'Dictionary', write a brochure entry for your own school, emphasizing all of its attractive features and amenities.

Holiday Advertisements

Group work

1 Look in detail at the language of the advertisements. What do you notice about:
a) vocabulary
b) sentence length
c) paragraph length?

2 What persuasive writing techniques are used to attract customers? Make a note of these.

3 Which advertisement is most effective in attracting you to the destination, and why?

Written assignment

Write the script for a 90-second radio advertisement based on either the ad for Jersey or Western Ireland. Beneath your script, describe the voices, effects and music you would use, and explain the decisions you have made in preparing the adverts.

Postcard from Epcot

Pair work

1   It is probably true that although most people have never visited Disney World or Epcot, most know about them. Share any impressions you have, using these questions as starting-points.

☐   What is Epcot?

☐   What is there to do when you visit it?

☐   Why is it so popular?

2   Discuss this reaction to Clive James' article. Do you react as strongly to his cynical style of reporting?

'It's a very unfair report. Clive James doesn't want to visit in the first place; therefore he has already made his mind up to 'knock' Epcot. He happens to visit on a day when the technology breaks down; therefore he can't judge what Epcot is like for most visitors on most days when everything works perfectly.'

Group work

Discuss the advantages and disadvantages of theme parks – whether in Britain, Europe or the USA. List their positive points, e.g. their cleanliness and safety, and their disadvantages. Then organize a class debate based on this statement:

'The parks like Epcot and Euro Disney are actually harmful because they create an impression of a world that is artificial and geared up to fun without responsibility. The real world is not like this.'

Written assignments

1   If you have visited one of the Disney theme parks, write a response to Clive James' article stating your opinion. You can acknowledge both good and bad aspects of the place.

2   Clive James' report is entitled 'Postcard from Epcot'. Skim-read it again, noting down the main points he makes. Then summarize his report in a space which is exactly the size of a postcard, around 100 words. How has the original message altered with your rewriting? Are there ways in which your summary actually improves upon the original 'postcard'?

Betjemanesque

Pair work

Some people claim that their holiday begins as soon as they arrive at the railway station or airport. Others would say that this can be the worst part of the holiday, especially if there is a delay. What is your opinion? Do you enjoy the 'process' of travel itself or do you merely want to reach your destination?

2   Notice how Simon Rae writes the poem as if he is one of the tourists by using the words 'we' and 'us'. Try reading the poem as if the author were an outside observer by putting in the words 'they' and 'them' instead. How is the effect of the poem different?

3   The title of Simon Rae's poem may be a mystery to you. It refers to the English poet, John Betjeman, who is known particularly for his comic verse. Look at these two verses from Betjeman's poem, '*A Subaltern's* Love-song*'.

Miss J. Hunter Dunn, Miss J. Hunter Dunn,
Furnish'd and burnish'd by Aldershot sun,
What strenuous singles we played after tea,
We in the tournament – you against me!

Love-thirty, love-forty, oh! weakness of joy,
The speed of a swallow, the grace of a boy,
With carefullest carelessness, gaily you won,
I weak from your loveliness, Joan Hunter Dunn.

(* a subaltern is an army officer below the rank of captain)

Although the subjects of Betjeman's and Rae's poems are very different, what similarities can you see in their styles? Look in particular at: the poets' choice of vocabulary, use of rhythm and rhyme, the tone of the poems.

Written assignment

Think of a mode of travel you have experienced on holiday, e.g. coach, plane, train, etc. Write a vivid account of a homeward journey from arrival at the rail station, airport, etc. to arriving home. Pay particular attention to other people travelling with you. You might, like Simon Rae, wish to exaggerate some aspects of their behaviour. Write this account in the form of an entry from a travel diary. Again, you do not need to have travelled far to do this.

To the Sea

Pair work

1 What clues are there that the poem is set in the past? Make a note of these.

2 What features of the poem are 'typically English'? On your own, look specifically at the vocabulary and images Larkin uses. Compare your examples with those of your partner. What makes these features so 'English'?

Group work

How far do you agree or disagree with these statements? Pick out details from the poem to support your viewpoint.

☐ The poem is partly about a journey to the sea, partly a journey into the past.

☐ Larkin does not idealize the seaside – he shows its disadvantages as well as its pleasures.

☐ Larkin likes the fact that the seaside unites old and young.

☐ Larkin pokes mild fun at British people.

Written assignment

Why do you think people enjoy going to the seaside, whether in Britain or abroad? What is the attraction of the sea? Conduct a survey amongst friends and adults about whether or not they would choose holidays by the sea. Write up your results, using graphs to indicate participants' holiday preferences, in an informative essay.

Mountain Madness

Pair work

1 What, according to Dr John Collee, are the advantages and disadvantages of staying at the Everest View Hotel? Make a note of these.

2 Can you think of any reasons why anyone would want to stay at this hotel? Would you like to visit it?

3 Discuss what the author means by this statement: 'to travel anywhere without sparing the time to assimilate is to defeat the purpose of going anywhere'.

Written assignment

What, in your opinion, are the necessary requirements of a good hotel? List these requirements in rank order, and then write a paragraph explaining your decisions. In your explanation, you might comment on whether the Everest View Hotel fulfils any of your requirements.

Barracuda Breakfast

Pair work

1 How would you describe Kevin Pilley's attitude to the Jules Verne Lodge? Does he like or dislike the idea of the underwater hotel? How can you tell?
2 Put together a 30-second radio or television commercial to attract customers to the hotel. Stress its positive points and give examples of satisfied customers' comments to show how much fun it is to stay at the hotel. Use sound effects and music.

Written assignment

Choose your own unusual location, e.g. at the South Pole or on an old steam train, and write about the kind of hotel you would ideally open there. What would be the unique selling points of your hotel, i.e. why would people want to stay there? When you have decided on these key facts, think about any further amenities your hotel would offer and then write an advertisement for it to appear in a national newspaper. For some examples of holiday advertisements see pages 94–95.

Coming Home

Background notes

This section examines the way travelling abroad affects our attitude to where we live when we return. It also raises the question about how well we can feel fully at home when we live abroad.

Frank Barrett's article, *Reasons to be Cheerful*, reports the results of a survey into what *The Independent* newspaper readers miss most when away from home on holiday. Grace Nichols' poem examines the mixed feelings of resettling in a new home in a new country.

The violinist, Yehudi Menuhin, writes about his 'favourite places' in a feature from *The Guardian*'s Saturday travel section.

A more gloomy attitude to returning home is evident in Nick

Danziger's postscript to his book of travels *Beyond Forbidden Frontiers*. Much more positive is Frank Kusy's return to Britain after travels in India: he simply cannot wait to travel again.

Reasons to be Cheerful

Pair work

1   Look through the list of items that British people miss whilst abroad and pick out the three items which you most agree with. Add to these items any not mentioned that you would include in your personal list.
2   Look carefully at the items in the list. Which items are mentioned more than once? Are there any common themes or patterns?
3   What do the types of items mentioned tell you about the readership of *The Independent*?

Written assignment

Devise a survey of aspects of life people in your group miss when on holiday. Limit the number of questions you ask to about 5 or 6. Use graphs or charts to present your findings, comparing the answers given with those in Frank Barrett's article. Write a commentary on your results highlighting any differences and similarities in the two sets of results.

Wherever I Hang

Group work

1   Grace Nichols shows the two sides of her emotions as she leaves for a new home. Note down the advantages and disadvantages of the home she is leaving and the advantages and disadvantages for her of living in England.
2   What do you think Nichols means in the last line of the poem?
3   What is the effect of the dialect words in the poem, e.g. 'belaang'? For example, how do they help to show the poet's feelings of being caught between her old life and her new one?

Written assignment

Where would you finally like to make your home – near where you live now, elsewhere in this country, or abroad? Write a personal essay outlining your preference and explaining your choice.

My Favourite Places

Group work

1 Discuss your favourite place. Choose your words carefully to describe it to the others in the group so that you explain what precisely makes the place so special to you.

2 Yehudi Menuhin mentions several favourite places – Ninfa in Italy, a Greek island, America and England. What is it about each place that is special to him?

Do you agree with his suggestion that our favourite places change as we grow older? Test this by asking adults at home about their favourite places. Pool all the results in your group and compare what each adult has said. Is there a pattern in what younger people like and what we tend to look for as we grow older?

Written assignments

1 Write about a place in this country or abroad that is special to you. Think carefully about its attractions – is it the look and atmosphere that appeal to you? Or is it the memories you have of people and experiences in this place? Has it changed during any later visits? Try to convey the 'specialness' of the place in about 500 words.

2 What is your least favourite place? Again, what makes you dislike it so much – the look of the place or its associations? Write a 500-word article about it.

Beyond Forbidden Frontiers

Pair work

1 Make a note of the different factors that make Danziger discontented upon his return from Tibet, China and Afghanistan.

2 Discuss what Danziger means when he says, 'I have become a stranger to my previous world but at the same time remain an outsider in those countries which I journey through'. What does this suggest as one possible negative effect of travel?

Written assignment

The hostility which Danziger encounters on his return home is based on prejudice: people prejudge him by his clothes and his colour. Write about an occasion when you have also been subjected to prejudice, either because of appearance, gender or age. How did you react?

Postscript

Pair work

How would you describe Kusy's mood when he first arrives home? How does this change during the short extract?

Written assignment

Take a fresh look at your home. What do you value about it? What are your favourite and least favourite places? When is your favourite time at home? Write a tribute 'To Home'.

Extended Activities

1 'There are some moments in life which are like pivots around which your existence turns . . . ' (Robyn Davidson). For a number of writers, their travel experiences have a centrally important effect on their lives. Examine two of the extracts in this collection in detail, which show how the authors' lives appear to have been affected – for better or worse – by the process of travel.

2 Choose the piece of travel writing which you most enjoyed in this anthology and the one which you most disliked. Compare the two in detail, showing why you responded as you did.

3 Spend some time researching a particular city or area that interests, either at home or abroad. Collect as much information from as many sources as possible, e.g. travel guides/brochures, video clips, postcards, newspaper articles, adverts, photographs, fictional accounts, charity information leaflets. Plan and write an analytical essay on how the place or area you have chosen is represented through different media, using your collection to illustrate your main points.

4 'Some travel writing teaches us about other cultures; some teaches us about our own. But it always teaches us about ourselves.' What have you learnt, about other cultures, your own culture, and yourself, from any of the writers in this book?

5 'The disadvantage of travel writing is that it is so highly personal. We watch another person's experiences but we cannot finally *share* them because we were not there.' Do you agree that travel writing is less easy to identify with than other forms, such as fiction? Illustrate your answer with reference to two or three of the writers in this anthology and refer to other forms of writing, if appropriate.

6 Does this anthology highlight any differences between being a male traveller and a female traveller? What different problems does gender bring, if any? Compare the accounts of two or three writers.

7 The danger with travel writing is that it encourages people to visit previously undiscovered places, thereby perhaps spoiling them, and often destroying the natural environment in the process. Do you think travel writers have any responsibility to prevent an influx of visitors?

8 Writer Paul Fussell says that the explorer seeks the undiscovered; the traveller seeks that which has been discovered; the tourist that which has been discovered by business and mass publicity: 'If the explorer moves towards the risks of the formless and the unknown, the tourist moves towards the security of pure cliché' (*Abroad*: page 39).

Choose one writer from each category and present a written account of what qualities make each one an explorer, traveller or tourist. Which of these forms of travel writing did you most enjoy? Why?

9   Undertake a survey of the different methods of travel used by other people in your class during the past month. They might range from plane journeys to skateboarding. Think of a way of measuring the advantages and disadvantages for each form of travel listed (for example, the possibility of long airport delays or damage done to the environment) and write the results up in a 'Guide to Travelling'.

Wider Reading

Assignments

Choose two (or more) of the books from the wider reading booklist which suit your own interest in travel writing. Read them and then use the assignment suggestions as guides for further work.

1   Examine the work of two writers who describe what it is like to move to new lives in Britain, e.g. Caryl Phillips or Jean Rhys; or who write about going to live permanently abroad, e.g. Gerald Durrell and Peter Mayle.

2   Some writers travel abroad to observe the customs of other people, e.g. Colin Thubron. How successfully do such writers convey the sense of a different and often remote life-style? Do they avoid patronizing the people they are describing?

3   Travel writing is sometimes a form of autobiography or confession, e.g. Robyn Davidson or Nick Danziger. Think about the idea that 'we travel in order to know ourselves better' and compare two writers in the light of the statement.

4   Compile your own travel anthology based on your reading. Decide how you will arrange the travel pieces you choose and whether you will illustrate the text with artwork and/or photos. Write a brief introduction to your collection explaining your decisions.

5   Compare the book and film versions of a travel story. For example, read E. M. Forster's *A Room with a View* and compare it with the film version. What are the strengths and weaknesses of each medium?

Booklist

The Art of Travel

Clive Brooks ed., *Life on the Liners*, Brooks Books, 1990.
Paul Fussell, *Abroad: British Literary Travelling Between the Wars*, OUP, 1980.
R. Price ed., *Life on the Airliners*, Brooks Books, 1991.

Explorers

Nigel Barley, *The Innocent Anthropologist*, Penguin, 1986; *A Plague of Caterpillars*, Penguin, 1987.
Isabella Bird, *A Lady's Life in the Rocky Mountains* (1879), Virago, 1982.

Annie Dillard, *Teaching a Stone to Talk*, Picador, 1984.
Lucy Duff-Gordon, *Letters from Egypt* (1865), Virago, 1983.
Graham Greene, *Journey Without Maps*, (1936), Penguin, 1971.
Charles Hose, *The Field-Book of a Jungle-Wallah* (1929), OUP 1985.
Robin Knox-Johnson, *A World of My Own*, Grafton, 1969.
Freya Stark, *A Winter in Arabia* (1940), Century, 1983.
A. F. Tschiffely, *Southern Cross to Pole Star* (1932), Century, 1982.

Travellers

Bill Bryson, *The Lost Continent: Travels in Small Town America*, Abacus, 1990.
The Best of Granta Travel, Granta Books, 1991.
William Cobbett, *Rural Rides* (1830), Penguin, 1985.
Bruce Chatwin, *What Am I Doing Here?*, Picador, 1990.
Nick Danziger, *Danziger's Travels*, Paladin, 1988.
Davies and Jansz, eds., *Women Travel: Adventures, Advice and Experience* in the Rough Guide series, Harrap Columbus, 1990.
Robyn Davidson, *Tracks*, Granada, 1982.
Christina Dodwell, *A Traveller on Horseback: in Eastern Turkey and Iran*, Sceptre, 1988.
Georgina Harding, *In Another Europe: A Journey to Romania*, Sceptre, 1990.
Clive James, *Flying Visits*, Picador, 1984.
Amryl Johnson, *Sequins for a Ragged Hem*, Virago, 1988.
Frank Kusy, *Kevin and I in India*, Impact Books, 1986.
Patrick Leigh Fermour, *The Traveller's Tree: A Journey Through the Caribbean Islands* (1950), Penguin, 1984.
Peter Mayle, *A Year in Provence*, Pan, 1990.
Jan Morris, *Journeys*, OUP, 1985.
Charles Nicholls, *Borderlines*, Picador, 1988.
Eric Newby, *A Traveller's Life*, Picador, 1983; *A Short Walk in the Hindu Kush*
Redmond O'Hanlon, *Into the Heart of Borneo*, Penguin, 1985.
Michael Palin, *Around the World in Eighty Days*, BBC Books, 1989.
Jonathan Raban, *Hunting Mr Heartbreak*, Picador, 1991.
Marsha Rowe, ed., *So Very English*, Serpent's Tail, 1991.
Mark Shand, *Travels on My Elephant*, Cape, 1991.
Lisa St Aubin de Terán, *Off the Rails: Memoirs of a Train Addict*, Sceptre, 1989.
Annabel Sutton, *The Islands in Between: Travels in Indonesia*, Impact Books, 1989.

Paul Theroux, *Sunrise with Sea Monsters*, Penguin, 1986; *Riding the Iron Rooster*, Penguin, 1988.
Colin Thubron, *Behind the Wall*, Penguin, 1988.
Tom Vernon, *Fat Man on a Bicycle*; *Fat Man in Argentinia*, Penguin, 1991.
Gavin Young, *Slow Boats to China*, Penguin, 1983.

Travel in Fiction*

Nigel Barley, *The Coast*, Penguin, 1991.
Peter Benson, *The Levels*, Penguin, 1987; *A Lesser Dependancy*, Penguin, 1990.
William Boyd, *A Good Man in Africa*, Penguin, 1982; *Stars and Bars*, Penguin, 1984; *Brazzaville Beach*, Penguin, 1991.
J. L. Carr, *A Month in the Country*, Harvester, 1990.
Sebastian Faulks, *The Girl at the Lion D'Or*, Vintage, 1990.
E. M. Forster, *A Room with a View* (1905), Penguin, 1955.
William Golding, *Rites of Passage*, *Close Quarters*, *Fire Down Below*, Faber, 1982, 1988, 1990.
Garrison Keillor, *Lake Wobegone Days*, Faber, 1987.
Garry Kilworth, *In the Shadow of the Deep-Sea Wave*, Unwin Hyman, 1989.
Caryl Phillips, *The Final Passage*, Faber, 1985.
Jean Rhys, *The Wide Sargasso Sea* (1966), Penguin, 1968.
Lisa St Aubin de Terán, *Slow Train to Milan*, Penguin, 1984.
Paul Theroux, *The Mosquito Coast*, Penguin, 1981.
Jules Verne, *Around the World in Eighty Days* (1872), Puffin Classics, 1990.
*Some titles are included for their strong evocation of place rather than the process of travel.